D0506349

# TRAINING
# GUNDOGS

# TRAINING
# GUNDOGS

## TONY JACKSON

WARD LOCK LIMITED · LONDON

## Acknowledgments

The author and publishers wish to thank Dick Mumford for his invaluable assistance with the photography; Peter Loughran for taking the photographs; Philip Murphy for the line drawings; and Gordon Carlisle (pages 77 and 88) and John Marchington (pages 32 and 89) for additional illustrations.

© Tony Jackson 1983

First published in Great Britain in 1983 by Ward Lock Limited, 82 Gower Street, London WC1E 6EQ, a Pentos Company.

Layout by Bob Swan
House editor Helen Douglas-Cooper

Text set in 11/12 pt Melior by Fakenham Photosetting Limited Fakenham, Norfolk

Printed and bound in Great Britain by Hollen Street Press Ltd, Slough, Berkshire

### British Library Cataloguing in Publication Data

Jackson, Tony
    Training gundogs.
    1. Hunting dogs    2. Dogs—Training
    I. Title
    636.7'52    SF428.5

    ISBN  0–7063–6251–9

# Contents

# Introduction

This book is intended for the man or woman who has never trained – perhaps has never even contemplated training – a gundog for practical work in the field. If you have already trained one or two dogs, you will probably know all about it . . . or think you do! Its aim is to enable you and your dog to achieve a level of competence that will make you an asset on a day's shooting. Then, if you wish to develop your abilities further, you can plunge into the world of field trials, and absorb all the literature on the subject from the masters of the trial world.

The interest in shooting, hunting and fishing continues to grow. Shooting is, in many parts of the country, almost oversubscribed, and there is enormous scope for competent gundogs and their handlers. There is always a demand for useful, working dogs, particularly in the field of picking-up. Although you may have no desire to carry a gun yourself, you can be of vital assistance on a shoot, helping to pick the slain, and there is also great scope in the world of tests and trials as ancillary activities.

The theme of this book is common sense. All gundog training revolves round this simple word, yet it is perhaps the most neglected aspect of training where the beginner is concerned. If only the novice trainer would try to see things from the dog's point of view instead of his own, progress and understanding would advance more rapidly.

# 1   The vital link

The decision to shoot live quarry is not one that can be undertaken lightly. In an age when every human activity comes under close scrutiny, those who shoot, whether game, wildfowl or rabbits, must at all times ensure that they adopt the highest possible code of ethics. Field sports, however, impose on the participant a number of obligations which must be accepted in full, a stricture which applies to the shooting of live quarry to a greater extent than in either hunting or fishing.

If you have decided that shooting is for you, you must be prepared to undertake two positive actions. First you must take shooting lessons to ensure that you are capable of handling a gun with maximum safety, and that you can bring a reasonable degree of skill to the shooting of live quarry. Second you must acquire a gundog; not just any gundog, but a reasonably competent companion which will serve you for perhaps eight or nine years. To shoot without the assistance of a capable gundog is not only a waste of time, but also potentially cruel. However, if you are invited to a day's driven pheasant, partridge or grouse shooting, you can be confident that the host will have arranged for professional pickers-up. You should leave to them the task of ensuring that every bird is collected, dead or wounded, so that you can concentrate on the shooting without the distraction of a dog at your side. What is more, one too often sees guns standing by their pegs with dogs either anchored to the ground, or tied to the guns' waists. In either case, the dog is a nuisance, and even a positive danger, distracting the gun from the business in hand.

The well-trained gundog, depending on its breed, is capable of fulfilling a variety of functions and is invariably an uncritical and ever-faithful companion. Apart from the formal driven shoot, there is no shooting occasion when a gundog is not a vital piece of equipment to the man or woman actively shooting. Let us take a look at some of the tasks facing the average gundog and see just how important a role it plays.

You may be walking a rough piece of meadow, dotted with clumps of thistle and weedy tussocks, for the odd rabbit. You shoot a couple while they are bolting towards the nearby hedge. Both are killed as clean as a whistle; a third bunny makes a dash for it but you are slow with the first barrel and hit it behind with the second. The rabbit struggles to the hedge and vanishes into a bury. One rabbit lost and likely to die in agony. If you had taken a dog with you, it would have picked the rabbit before it made the hedge and retrieved it to you with the minimum of fuss.

Perhaps you are shooting pigeon over decoys. You may have killed a dozen or so, but then you wing one which flutters into a spinney 300 metres away; a lost bird unless you have a dog.

And if you are wildfowling, you will only go once without a dog. A good flight of teal or wigeon with dead or wounded birds bobbing away on the tide or lost on the other side of a sea-filled gutter, will teach you that a dog is the essential third part of a shooting team – man, gun and dog.

The role of the dog in sport is a long and honourable one; a development of those far-off days when the dog was an essential instrument in man's survival. Hounds were used to chase and hold at bay or pull down deer and wild boar, rabbits and hares. In later centuries, a small reddish dog would lure duck into the decoy-man's funnel nets, while cocker spaniels have in the past been used to flush game into strategically-placed nets.

As the gun was developed through the ages, from firelock to matchlock, flintlock, percussion and breechloader, so too was the use of dogs in the sport, to match its wider application. Sporting shooting took off in the eighteenth century when 'shooting flying' became normal practice instead of a curious and happy fluke. The flintlock muzzle-loader became lighter, better balanced and swifter in its mechanical action. It was then the practice to walk the scythe-cut, knee-high stubbles for partridges, shooting over pointers or perhaps taking on pheasants, woodcock, duck or snipe flushed by a spaniel.

This was to be the calm, unaltered pattern for many years, the only change being a switch in the means of ignition from flint to percussion cap. Those peaceful autumn days of pointers or setters locked fast on to the coveys of grey partridges, of rolling clouds of black powder smoke, and of a leisurely pace were, however, doomed. With the importation of the battue from Europe, the initially much-scorned driving of semi-tame pheasants, and the invention of the breechloader, the golden days were to vanish. The reign of the pointers, setters and spaniels was to be eclipsed as driven shooting became standard practice. As shooting changed, and the hitherto game-beneficial and less productive agricultural practices were superseded, so the demand for gundogs capable of a very different type of work increased. The days of the slow and pottering spaniels, the field, Clumber and Sussex, were over. Pace, style and retrieving ability became all-important. The era of the flatcoat, golden retriever and the breed which was eventually to eclipse both, the labrador retriever, had arrived. The English springer spaniel, thanks to its versatility, maintained its status, to become a serious rival in popularity to the labrador.

Between World War I and World War II, and for perhaps two decades after World War II, labradors and English springers dominated the gundog world; the former acted as the perfect no-slip retriever, the ideal companion for the game shot who demanded a dog that could mark, hunt intelligently at a distance and retrieve tenderly to hand, whilst the springer combined these virtues with the ability to hunt within shot. They have markedly dissimilar temperaments, the one placid and willing to work at a moderate pace, the other a contained bundle of energy which demands to be controlled.

You should take your own temperament into account when considering which breed of gundog to choose. On the whole, if you tend to be highly strung and easily excited, you will probably discover a close rapport with springers, whereas the man or woman who takes life at a slower and more reflective pace will find the labrador more suited to his or her moods. Of course, it does not always work out like that!

In the next chapter we will discuss the choice of a gundog in depth, a choice which, in the last few years, has broadened considerably. No longer does one think automatically in terms of either a labrador or a springer. New faces have emerged on to the gundog scene, a healthy and invigorating sign, which will be of great benefit to the gundog world and to the shooting man.

Whatever your choice of breed, and there is no reason to stick rigidly to one breed, one thing is very certain. Long after you have finally retired your gun there will still be a gundog by your fireplace, a dreaming companion whose presence can stir a wealth of happy memories. Many shooting men and women, understanding that dogwork is by far the more exciting and complicated part of shooting, will eventually happily put the gun aside to pick-up for their fellow guns.

I have emphasized that the acquisition of a gundog is essential if the shooting man is to be complete, but do not undertake the commitment lightly. You will be entering a new way of life, one from which there is no escape.

# 2   The choice of breed

There are a number of breeds to choose between, due to a growing interest in, and desire to investigate, breeds that have until recently been overshadowed and dominated by the labrador and springer. The golden retriever, its field attributes kept alive by a handful of sound working kennels, has of late made considerable inroads into the practical gundog scene, being particularly successful in trials. And this despite its emergence as a show and pet dog. It is fair to say that the show world has been the ruination of breed after breed of working dog; so much so, that today the show springer, for instance, is physically a totally different animal from its working cousin, and quite incapable of performing its original function.

The field spaniel is a typical case in point. Before World War I, breeders decided that short legs and long backs were desirable. Dogs at shows were stretched out to make them appear as long as possible with the result that crooked legs and sagging backs became common. From being a practical shooting companion, the field spaniel became quite useless.

Today, with the possible exception of the hunt-point-retrieve breeds, such as the German short-haired pointer, vizsla and weimaraner, a potential gundog owner would be well advised to steer clear of the slightest hint of show blood. This can swiftly be discovered by examination of the pedigrees of the sire and dam, to see if Sh. Ch. appears in front of a name – and make sure you do so!

Regrettably, there is much backyard breeding, based on scant knowledge of genetics or bloodlines and, often, a desire to 'have a litter from the old girl ... there's a nice dog up the road', and the country is awash with dubious, badly-bred dogs. This too is a pitfall you must avoid at all costs.

First, you should study the breeds available in relation to your type of shooting. Choice of a dog is very personal, and frequently irrational, and although I can point you in various directions, show you the dangers to avoid and the snags you may encounter, at the end of the day you may choose a dog that, on the face of it, appears totally unsuitable for the work ahead. Never mind, if you like that breed and feel you have a rapport with it, go ahead.

Gundogs can be divided into four divisions: there are the retrievers, headed by the labrador and followed closely in terms of popularity by the golden retriever, then the flatcoat; there are the spaniels, the English springer being way out in front, the cocker and the Welsh springer trailing behind; there are the pointers and setters, which are too specialized for beginners; and lastly there are the up-and-coming breeds, the hunt-point-retrievers (HPRs), namely the German short-haired pointer, the weimaraner, the vizsla and the large Munsterlander.

Each division has its specialized work, but obviously there is a degree of overlapping. The labrador is the retrieving specialist, the springer the hunter *par excellence*, and the setter and pointer are intended to point their quarry. The HPR breeds are expected to perform all three functions, but without, perhaps, the degree of competence exhibited by the specialists. HPRs are really maids-of-all-work and a degree of compromise must be accepted.

## The retrievers
The choice of a breed is closely linked to the work it will be expected to perform. If, for instance, you are going to crawl the mud-flats below the high-water mark, or intend to undertake a considerable amount of inland duck shooting, the labrador is the breed you should have, without doubt. It is still the most popular dog in the shooting field, but the old-fashioned type of labrador, strong of bone with a heavy head, waterproof double coat and a great thick pole of a tail, is seldom seen today. But if you can find one you will not have call for a better water dog. The origin of the labrador is not clear, but it is believed that the first specimens were obtained from seafarers plying between Newfoundland and Poole, Dorset, in the early part of the nineteenth century. The subsequent history of the breed has been carefully recorded. Its gentle and adaptable nature has ensured it a pre-eminent position with working gundog and pet owners alike; and it is still the most popular choice as a guide dog for the blind.

Sadly, hereditary diseases, chiefly hip-dysplasia and retinal

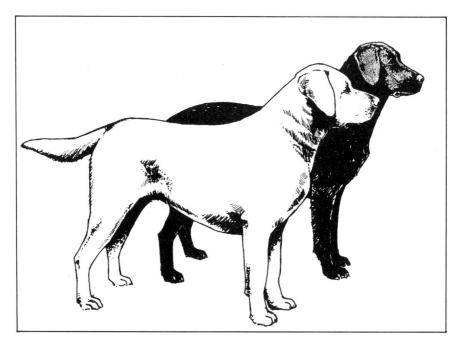

*Labrador retriever.*

atrophy, are now rife in the breed, and it is vital to make sure, when buying a puppy, that *both* parents are certified free from disease. Be adamant about this. However appealing the pup and beguiling its pedigree, do not consider purchasing it unless this condition can be met. Again and again, one hears sad stories of young labradors, perhaps under a year old, that have had to be destroyed because their hips were deformed. Until the breed can be certified free from these two diseases—and that is a long way off—the future of the labrador must be in doubt. There are also many small, thin-faced labradors; dogs that bear little resemblance to the old-fashioned stalwart type. This is not to say that they do not do their work adequately, they can make excellent gundogs, but they no longer resemble the labrador of former days.

The duties of the labrador in the game field are to remain free from chase, to walk at heel, mark shot game, retrieve to hand and, if necessary, sit while game is driven over the guns. In the less formal atmosphere of the rough shoot, it may also be expected to hunt cover, but with rather less of the jungle-busting drive of the springer spaniel. However, the labrador is really in his element on the foreshore. Being a powerful swimmer, he will retrieve a heavy goose across hundreds of metres of glutinous mud, and bear the most bitter conditions with exemplary fortitude.

Golden retrievers are now seen with increasing regularity in the shooting field and their duties are exactly the same as those of the labrador; though with their long coat, they never look comfortable on the foreshore. Goldies are slow to mature, a point that must be taken into consideration, for a greater degree of patience will be required during training, before the polished end-product is seen.

The flatcoat retriever had its heyday during the Golden Age of shooting, those late-Victorian and Edwardian years of untroubled peace and perambulating house-parties. It has been described as a charming, sporting Edwardian with great intelligence, seldom sulking and always prepared for fun.

Owners who have had the pleasure of working flatcoats have

*Golden retriever.*

*Flatcoat retriever.*

almost invariably sworn by the breed. Easily trained, brave and intelligent it is now, sadly, finding favour with the show world, which can only lead to the decline of the breed as a working force. Fortunately the incidence of disease appears to be lower than it is among labradors.

Of the four breeds of retriever, the curly-coat is the least familiar. A big, powerful dog, weighing 30–35 kg (70–80 lb), its astrakhan-like coat of crisp, tight curls frequently misleads the unknowing into supposing it to be a 'sort of poodle', or a cross with an Irish water spaniel. In fact, whilst its origins are obscure, it may well be that the water spaniel played some part in its ancestry. In the seventeenth edition of *British Rural Sports* by Stonehenge (1888), it is recorded that, 'The modern retriever ... is now almost always a cross – that of the setter and Newfoundland showing the smooth wavy coat and that of the water spaniel (generally Irish) with the Newfoundland having the coat curly'.

The curly-coat is described as having an affectionate nature com-

*Curly-coated retriever.*

bined with a droll sense of humour. In the field, an accomplished curly-coat is a powerful and efficient performer, revelling in particular in its natural element, water. A strong swimmer, it will quickly be discovered that the curly takes to water as a puppy without the slightest coercion.

The curly-coat reached the height of its popularity towards the end of the nineteenth century, and was greatly favoured by keepers, who appreciated it not only as a gundog but also as a guard-dog.

Today, the principal problem with working curlies is to obtain proven stock. There are only one or two kennels producing the curly-coat for work, the majority being show bred. It is a sad state of affairs and any encouragement that can be given to this handsome breed is to be welcomed.

A notable point in favour of the curly-coat is that the tightly curled coat does not shed hairs, and it requires only a minimum of grooming apart from the removal of burrs, seeds and thorns.

## The spaniels

Now let us take a close look at the spaniels. There is a choice of seven working breeds available in Great Britain, but inspection will quickly reveal that the field can be narrowed down to three practical workers, two borderlines and two non-starters. In order of merit these are, way out in front, the English springer spaniel, the cocker spaniel and the Welsh spaniel, followed by the Irish water spaniel and the Clumber, and lastly the field and Sussex spaniels. Doubtless, lovers of the last four named would dispute their placing!

Without doubt or quibble, the English springer spaniel leads the spaniel field in terms of working ability and versatility. Yet its emergence as a leading star in the practical gundog world is comparatively recent, while its history is shrouded in a relative degree of obscurity. It was only in 1902 that the Kennel Club recognized the English springer as a breed; its parentage appears to have been a cocktail of cocker blood, the so-called Norfolk spaniel and probably an infusion of blood from a line of spaniels which had been kept

*English springer spaniel.*

pure since 1800 by a family in Shropshire. Certainly, there is no mention in Stonehenge's book, from which I quoted earlier, of any spaniel resembling an English springer, the Clumbers, Sussex, Norfolk, Welsh and cocker spaniels then being pre-eminent.

The contemporary English springer is divided into two distinct types: show and working. There is enormous disparity between the physical appearance of the two types; the show springer is a ponderous, narrow-headed, heavily feathered creature with long, drooping ears. The working springer is neat and alert, with a broad head, short ears and a minimum of feathering. In other words, it is built for pace and drive, qualities matched by its keen mental abilities. Once again, it should be emphasized that it is very important to obtain working blood when picking a puppy. Show lines should be avoided at all cost.

The prime purpose of a spaniel is to hunt for game within comfortable range of the gun. It should be capable of dealing with all types of cover from the thickest brambles and reeds to bracken and hedgerows. The working springer is expected to make good every inch of its ground, so that the gun can be confident that neither he nor the dog have walked over a tucked-up rabbit or pheasant. The dog is expected to drop or at least stand to shot and retrieve on order. Good springers appear to be just as at home in water as labradors, but they are out of place on the foreshore. For the rough shooter prepared to cope with its bustling energy and buzzing dynamo, the English springer is an obvious choice. It is a particularly kind dog, and well suited to living indoors as a friend of the family.

The cocker spaniel is not merely a scaled-down version of the springer. It is a breed, or in the early days a type, of considerable antiquity. A form of spaniel was mentioned in chronicles of the tenth century, and in the Prologue to the Wife of Bath's Tale by Chaucer (1340–1400) there is mention of a spaniel. The name cocker may derive from its use over the centuries, particularly in Wales, to flush woodcock into nets.

Weighing in the region of 12–13.5 kg (28–30 lb), the cocker is a compact spaniel that tends to contain within its small frame a very distinctive sense of humour or, as some trainers would call it, devilment. It is definitely not a dog for the beginner.

The springer and cocker each take a different approach to finding game; the former choosing to work out a piece of cover assiduously, whilst the latter prefers to have definite evidence that game is present.

*Cocker spaniel.*

While it is true that cockers have had a bad, and probably justified, press in the past, the working cocker has made considerable advances in recent years, thanks in part to the dedication of men like Keith Erlandson, who have been prepared to pick up the challenge posed by these merry little devils. Good working cockers are in considerable demand, as kennels producing reliable strains are few and far between.

Another spaniel with a long and respectable history is the handsome red-and-white Welsh springer. Half way between a cocker and an English springer in size, the Welshman appears to have originated in Glamorgan, where strains were kept pure for many years, apart from a possible introduction of Brittany blood.

It is sad that although a really good Welsh springer is a pleasure to work, such dogs are few and far between. The Welshman has a tendency to hunt a line rather than cover its beat, and its retrieving can, in certain cases, be suspect. Finding a good Welshman is difficult today, but if you are fortunate enough to come across one, you

*Welsh springer spaniel.*

will be the lucky owner of, perhaps, the most handsome of the spaniel tribe. Its dark-red and gleaming-white coat is distinctive.

The Irish water spaniel is, without doubt, a genuine individual in the gundog world. It is a dog remarkable to behold, with a delightful temperament, and if you can obtain a good one, it will be a diligent worker. There is some doubt as to whether the Irishman is a spaniel at all. Descended from a long line of water dogs, it became established in Ireland in the nineteenth century, a Mr Justin McCarthy founding the present line of dogs with a stud dog called Boatswain.

The Irish water spaniel has a distinctive coat of small tight curls, a slender, round tail, a top-knot of curls and a smooth face with a dark-brown, medium-sized eye. The coat gives off a distinctive odour unless the dog is groomed regularly. Grooming is vitally important with this breed, otherwise the liver-coloured, curly coat will become a tangled matt of dead hair. The Irishman is devoted to water, its tightly-curled, slightly oily coat protecting it from the fiercest cold and most miserable conditions.

21

*Irish water spaniel.*

Very much an individual, it will respond to thoughtful training with alacrity and to kindness with a ready response. It is perhaps sad that working kennels are few and far between, and that, as a result, the Irishman is only occasionally seen in the field. It is slow to mature, and is well worth the wait.

The resemblance to the spaniel tribe is slight and while there is doubtless spaniel blood in its background, a strong infusion of poodle, and probably setter, has set this dog apart.

The Clumber spaniel is, sadly, one of the borderline cases. A massive-framed dog and immensely strong, its pace is considerably slower than the springer or cocker. It is probable that the breed was introduced into this country at the end of the eighteenth century, by the second Duke of Newcastle to his estate at Clumber Park, he having received the dogs as a gift from a Frenchman, the Duc de Noilles. However, this is by no means an established fact. It has also been suggested that a cross between the old English spaniel and the

French bassett could have resulted in the Clumber, though this seems unlikely. The original kennels were all centred in Nottinghamshire; kennels such as Welbeck, Osberton Hall and, of course, Clumber Park.

The Clumber was in its heyday as a working dog in the last years of the nineteenth and early years of the twentieth centuries. It enjoyed a brief resurgence of popularity when King George V encouraged the breed, having discovered that its slow-paced, methodical method of hunting was ideally suited to the rhododendron coverts at Sandringham.

The Clumber is indeed large for a spaniel, a dog weighing 27–31 kg (60–70 lb), a bitch 20–27 kg (45–60 lb). It is predominantly white in colour, with lemon or orange markings; the head is square and broad, while the deep stop and heavy muzzle give it a somewhat thoughtful expression.

It is encouraging to note that the working Clumber has not entirely been forgotten. A handful of owners are doing their utmost to

*Clumber spaniel.*

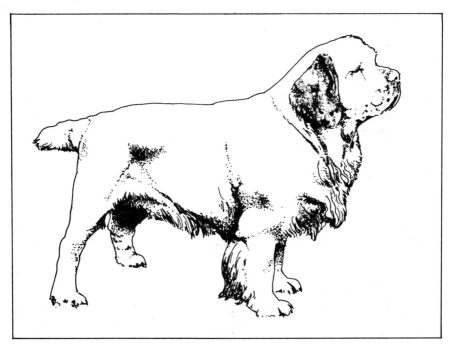

improve the breed for the field. There is still, as they would be the first to admit, a long way to go before the Clumber becomes a serious contestant as a practical working gundog, but the very fact that a field trial was held for the breed in 1982 clearly indicates that this large, old-fashioned character may have a future.

We come, sadly, to the two breeds of spaniel which, today, can scarcely be given serious consideration as practical gundogs. The field spaniel evolved in the early years of the nineteenth century, and doubtless in its ancestry contained a mixture of cocker, Norfolk and Sussex blood. A line of solid, liver-coloured dogs was eventually established. Heavily built, with a deep chest and today a compact appearance, the field was formerly used in thick cover and, being docile and easy to train, it made a useful companion. Sadly, changing styles of shooting, and in particular the attentions of the show bench, brought to a close this breed's practical career. By the early 1900s, the fashion for long backs and low legs had produced a creature which was almost deformed. It would be hard to suggest

*Field spaniel.*

*Sussex spaniel.*

where, today, one might find a genuine and effective working kennel.

The Sussex spaniel is of a golden liver shade, and is a strong dog with a wide skull, in appearance not unlike a small Clumber. The breed has been known for about 150 years and at one time was very popular in shooting circles. It has two odd traits: a curious rolling gait, though this is perhaps less often seen today; and a habit of giving tongue when hunting. Originally well up on the leg, the show world demanded a short-legged creature, one which would no longer be able to hunt in thick cover, its prime purpose.

### The hunt–point–retrieve breeds

Now we come to the recent additions to the practical gundog world in Great Britain, the hunt–point–retrieve breeds. These comprise the leader of the group, the German short-haired pointer (GSP), the weimaraner and the vizsla. These breeds, emanating from continental Europe, have made their mark in this country since World War II. Many servicemen saw them at work during, and in the years immediately after, that war and were so captivated by their obvious attributes that they imported specimens to this country.

I must here admit my own interest. I have owned labradors and English springers, all of which I have worked under a variety of conditions from the foreshore to the covert. I have enjoyed and liked them all but I confess that I have been totally converted to German short-haired pointers.

The GSP is a large, cleanly-built dog weighing around 23–30 kg (50–70 lb) and the colour is usually liver-flecked, though black-and-white or solid liver is also encountered. The tail is docked to two-fifths of its original length.

Originating from continental Europe in the seventeenth century, the dogs were designed not for a specific task but to be all-purpose dogs, capable of hunting, pointing game, retrieving, tracking, swimming and also hunting deer.

With its clean, smooth coat, which does not shed hair, its gentle disposition and intelligence, the GSP makes an ideal companion in the field or house.

*German short-haired pointer.*

The breed is now becoming so popular as a working gundog in Britain, it is threatening to replace the hitherto ubiquitous labrador as the number one gundog. Fortunately the breed is disease-free at the moment, and as a great number of show dogs are worked this situation is likely to prevail until the breed is 'taken up' by the show bench; they will doubtless prefer light-boned, elegant dogs that will eventually have the working strength bred out of them.

Its detractors claim that the German shorthaired pointer is hard-mouthed. This is a gross libel; certainly there are GSPs with jaws like rat-traps, but that fault is not unknown amongst other breeds as well! A tendency to hard-mouth is almost invariably the fault of the trainer. As youngsters, and certainly in their first working season, they must not be allowed to pick up runners or wounded birds.

As far as water is concerned, there may be some hesitancy in the first year, but once the dog has matured the element holds no terrors for it. These dogs tend to mature later than labradors or springers, and one must bear with them, and understand their juvenile approach to life until the penny drops.

My GSP was trained in the company of a middle-aged spaniel and this ensured that the thickest cover held no fear for him. He would simply follow the spaniel, assuming that the other knew what he was up to!

The beginner may wonder how to teach the dog to point. There is really no cause for worry here. You will discover that pointing is programmed into the animal's circuitry. Initially it will point almost anything—field mice, meadow-pipits, larks—but as it grows older it will come to distinguish right from wrong.

The weimaraner, sometimes known as the grey ghost, is a handsome, clean-limbed dog whose history is complicated. It is claimed that the dog has developed without outcrosses of blood and that, in particular, pointer blood is lacking. This school holds to the theory that the Benedictine monks in the Ardennes, as long ago as the ninth century, fixed the breed by mating two black dogs of the St Hubertus Brachen, the resulting grey colour of the offspring setting the standard.

Suffice to know that the breed took its name from the town of Weimar, capital of the State of Thuringia, where it prospered under the encouraging eye of the Grand Duke Karl August, Duke of Saxe-Weimar-Eisenbach, who died in 1828.

The breeding of the weimaraner has been carefully controlled and it was not until the early 1950s that the first dogs appeared in Britain.

*Weimaraner.*

Heralded as a new wonder-dog, the breed received initial and understandable hostility, but eventually proved itself as a useful gundog. Weimaraners are inclined to hunt closely, acknowledging points at close range; good jumpers and superb in water, they are also excellent on wounded game, bringing their wonderful hunting abilities into play. Regrettably, the breed has been split between show and work, though conformation remains the same; undoubtedly working ability on the show side is in decline.

The Hungarian vizsla, a reddish-golden dog, emanates, as its name suggests, from Hungary. Like the two hunt–point–retrieve breeds just discussed, it is expected to perform all three jobs from land and water.

The vizsla has a curious temperament, an odd mixture of timidity and fearlessness, which tends to make it difficult to train, but once the secret has been mastered it is a quite delightful dog with a strong sense of humour. Vizslas are all too easily cowed if roughly treated, but their sense of stubborn determination requires an equal deter-

*Hungarian vizsla.*

mination on the part of the trainer. Vizslas are intensely loyal dogs, a streak which seems to run right through the HPR breeds. They all tend to be 'one-man' dogs, acknowledging the presence of strangers but single-minded of purpose where their owner and handler is concerned.

Vizslas are far happier living in the house, where they also make excellent guard dogs. Demanding affection, they will return it in full. They are attractively handsome, but do not lend themselves readily to training, and demand owners who can appreciate and relate to their individual character.

The English pointer and the Gordon, Irish and English setters have been ignored deliberately. They are specialist breeds and therefore are quite unsuitable for the novice gundog owner. They need to be used in wide, open country if their potential is to be realized. Today, pointers and setters are used almost exclusively on grouse moors and, with the increase in dogging, due largely to the rising cost of driving, pointers and setters are making a comeback. They are, however, dogs for the specialist and need not be considered here.

# 3 Picking a puppy

There are four methods of obtaining a dog intended for work in the field. You can purchase a puppy with the intention of training it yourself, and this is by far the most popular method. You can buy a youngster, into which the basic training has been instilled, with a view to finishing its education. You can acquire a ready-trained dog. Or you can run on your puppy until, at seven, eight or nine months it is ready to be sent to a professional trainer, who will do the hard work for you.

Cost, time and, perhaps, the desire to prove that you can do it yourself play a decisive role. Obviously the cheapest method is to purchase a puppy and train it yourself, but you must be fully aware of what exactly will be demanded of you if you are to do justice to the pup, and to produce a companion which, even though it may not approach field trial standards, will nevertheless be efficient in its work and not cause you major embarrassments in the field. The dog that persistently runs in whenever a shot is fired, or a bird or rabbit flushed, and which then refuses to return is, quite simply, a sad reflection on its owner. The animal itself can hardly be blamed; it is the slack, weak discipline and sheer lack of training that has brought it to this pass.

Training a gundog to its role in life, with the caveat that it is a suitable breed for the work intended and chosen from working stock, is not an especially difficult task, provided that common sense rules the day.

You must decide whether the environment in which you live is suitable for training; that does not mean whether you live in a town or the country, but simply whether your family will co-operate in observing the rules of basic discipline. An understanding family is more important than being surrounded by fields! Many a good dog has been trained in a town; provided that there is accessible park-land, or that you have a short back lawn, there is no reason why you should not produce a satisfactory result. A good friend, who worked in London, took his young springer to town with him each day and provided it with basic discipline with a ten-minute session in Hyde Park every lunch hour.

Training your own youngster is, of course, far more satisfying than having to purchase the services of a third party to do the job for you. I would recommend it every time. You may feel that for finan-cial reasons there is no alternative; so be it, but do remember that common sense is the key to success.

Today a labrador, springer or GSP puppy will probably cost you between £70 and £100. That may sound a substantial sum, but you are purchasing a useful companion with a working life of, perhaps, ten years.

## Choose with care

Having decided on the breed of gundog you require, you must contact a breeder or kennels that has a reputation to maintain. Good, even excellent, dogs can be, and frequently are, bought through private hands and you may well be fortunate. Sadly, though, there are far too many litters produced today for no reason other than sentiment. Another collection of cuddly, charming pups is foisted onto the world. Was any thought given to the breeding on either side? Were both parents certified free from hip-dysplasia and retinal atrophy? It is worth waiting some time, up to a year and even longer, for a good litter to be produced.

To find a list of working kennels, you can consult the classified columns of the shooting magazines, or approach the secretary of the breed society of your choice. He or she will undoubtedly be able to point you in the right direction, and may even know of good litters available at the time.

Let us assume that you have chosen a breed of gundog, that you have found a breeder and are satisfied that the litter is of impeccable working strain and, most important, that the parents are certified free from disease. Do not be reticent about taking advice from knowledgeable gundog folk; the fact that they may be involved in field trials does not place them on a higher plane. You will discover that they are only too pleased to assist beginners, so listen to their advice, weigh it up and act upon it.

Picking a pup is fraught with problems. The selection of sex and

*The choice of puppy is always a gamble.*

colour is easily solved, but how on earth are you to choose a potential top-class working gundog from the wriggling, appealing,
squirming bundles, each as charming as its litter brothers and sisters? It is a gamble, and at the end of the day the puppy you select
will be the one that displays the right mixture of colour scheme and
appeal.

You can undertake certain simple tests. For instance, clap your
hands and note any pups which flinch at the sound; see the litter
running together and mark the bold pups; knot a handkerchief and
throw it, watching for the keen, interested retrievers. Open the
puppy's mouth and check that the bite is even; under- or over-shot
jaws are most definitely not required. If the puppies have done well,
they will have loose, glossy coats and will exude an air of well-
being.

Do not, even at the risk of domestic crisis, take any other members
of your family with you. You must make the decision, and you must
not allow yourself to be influenced in any way. Puppies of eight or so

weeks are incredibly appealing, and others are likely to succumb to sheer charm, ignoring the tell-tale signs that just *may* indicate a worker.

Be prepared for several nights of disturbance. You must realize that for the puppy, being removed from its litter siblings and dam is a traumatic experience. Try to provide warmth, comfort and kindness; and make sure that the breeder gives you the feeding instructions as adherence to these will provide some continuity in the puppy's life.

## A semi-trained dog

If you prefer to buy a young dog that has already received some basic groundwork, a dog that is between six and fifteen months old, you must obviously be prepared to pay considerably more. However, great care is called for, as dogs of this age are all too frequently kennel cast-outs, the animals which, in the breeder's view, are not going to make the grade. They may, of course, meet the requirements of a fairly undemanding shooting owner; equally, they may be seriously flawed.

If you choose to consider a semi-trained dog, it is essential that you watch the dog being demonstrated by the trainer. He will have made certain claims for it, and you should see that the animal does walk to heel, is not gun-shy, can undertake simple retrieves and, if a spaniel, is prepared to enter cover and hunt. Listen with care to the commands given and, if you choose to buy be sure that all the instructions, including whistle notes used, are written down. Continuity is the key-note to purchasing a half- or fully-trained dog. Make sure that you have the same whistle as the trainer, use the same commands and appreciate that the dog is not a robot. The fact that it will work for the trainer whom it knows and loves, does not mean that it will automatically perform the same functions for you ... not immediately, that is.

All too often, a new owner expects his acquisition to work the day after he has bought it, and to maintain the standards demonstrated. This is totally unfair to the dog, which may require several weeks to acclimatize to its new situation and to gain confidence. Once again, common sense plays a major role.

## The professional trainer

Much the same criteria apply if you decide to run the puppy for six or seven months, and then send it away to be trained. The most important point to remember is that you must contact your potential trainer well in advance. It is no use ringing up at the last moment and expecting him to take over. Some trainers prefer the raw article with a minimum of interference by the owner, while others are agreeable to basic training being instilled, such as walking to heel, answering to its name, and even some simple dummy work. The trainer will be able to assess the task facing him when he meets you and has a look at the pup.

What he will not need is spoiled goods. Do not imagine that he will go to the bother of trying to straighten out your mistakes: hard-mouth, gun-nerves, chase, refusing to retrieve. These errors are too frequently the fault of the amateur trainer, who then expects the unfortunate professional to sort out the mess. No, discuss your requirements in the very early stages and abide by the trainer's requests.

Training the dog may take up to six months, depending on the ability of the animal and the amount of time that the trainer can devote to it. You should also be aware that the trainer may agree to accept the dog only for a preliminary trial period. If, at the end of it, he chooses not to continue with training, that is his decision. You can rest assured that he will have very good reasons for rejecting the animal, and you should abide by his decision.

Once again you must be absolutely clear in your own mind that the dog, which has been under the close attention of its trainer for several weeks, at a period of its life when it is particularly receptive, will have shifted its loyalties. You must give the animal time to settle down before even contemplating working it and, of course, you will have observed the dog being worked by the trainer, noting carefully his commands, which must be duplicated.

**The soft option**
Finally, there is the soft option, the simple answer, provided your purse is sufficiently deep. You can buy a ready-made dog. Two important points must be borne in mind. The first is that a fully-trained gundog is not cheap—there is no reason why it should be. Perhaps eighteen months to two years old, a considerable amount of time and cash will have been expended to bring it to a desirable standard, so be prepared to pay £400–£500, or more. It may sound like a large amount of money, but a good dog, like a good horse, is a valuable commodity.

The ground rules for purchase remain virtually the same. Make extensive enquiries about the kennels or trainer from whom you are considering buying the dog; carefully check the animal's background, noting pedigree and taking care there is a disease-free certificate for both parents. See the animal demonstrated and mark with attention the handling methods. Do try to understand that you are not buying a machine that will perform automatically for you at the touch of a button. Expensive the dog may be, capable of performing more than adequately under its trainer, but that does not mean it will necessarily go well for you unless you give it a chance to become used to its new and strange environment. For a dog of whatever age, a new home and master is a traumatic wrench, which can be resolved only by time, patience and understanding.

Do not, under any circumstances, take the dog out shooting within a week or so of its arrival; take it for walks, establish a mutual affection and bond and then, when you feel the time is ripe, take it to a shoot, but do no more than pick-up. When you are satisfied that the dog is reacting to commands, take it out with the gun. You will need to sacrifice sport for the benefit of the dog; in other words, concentrate on the animal and act swiftly and firmly at the slightest indication of disobedience.

## Choice of sex
Whatever method you choose to obtain your gundog, the choice of sex is of paramount importance. It is frequently suggested that bitches are, on the whole, more biddable and easier to train, while dogs are headstrong and less amenable. Bitches have the disadvantage of coming into heat for three weeks twice a year. It is, undoubtedly, a very difficult time for the owner. All too often, such is Murphy's Law, she will come on heat in the middle of the shooting season or at some equally critical moment. If you do not wish to breed from her and have an aversion to cross-bred litters, the bitch must be held under lock and key.

If you do own a bitch, you can have her injected by your vet if she has been caught by a dog, but this must take place within a matter of hours and will upset the cycle of her heat—quite apart from the unnecessary cost.

On the other hand, you may decide that the problems associated with oestrus are balanced by the gentler nature of a bitch, and the fact that, if you wish, you can breed from her.

A dog will naturally be larger than a bitch, and will tend to be more headstrong and self-willed, though much depends on the

breed. Some dogs, and labradors in particular, are inclined to roam, especially if there is a bitch in season in the neighbourhood. Of course, ideally the dog should be kennelled and exercised only under supervision, but accidents can happen. A dog that strays will all too swiftly take to self-hunting, and once the forbidden delights of the local rabbits and game have been tasted, only the most stern and repressive measures will suppress this vice.

Whichever sex you decide on, it is best to purchase a puppy from a litter whelped in the late winter or early spring. You will then have the summer months to get to know each other, and whilst the youngster should most certainly not be entered to the shooting field the following season—in January it will be only nine to eleven months old—you will then have the following year to polish its performance ready for the next shooting season, and will also be able to work it on rabbits and pigeon in the summer months.

For the busy owner, probably fully occupied during the day, those summer months are essential if he or she is to do justice to the dog. Training sessions can take place after supper, and the first introduction to water will hold few terrors in the warm evenings.

## Innoculations

Before acquiring your puppy, you must find out from the breeder whether it has received any innoculations. If not, you must make an appointment with your vet in order to have it protected against the four principal diseases which affect dogs in Britain: distemper and hardpad, infectious hepatitis, and kidney and liver leptospirosis. You will receive a certificate from the vet, and instructions on the frequency of booster shots. Your vet, on whose advice you would be wise to rely implicitly, will also advise you on the distasteful subject of worms.

Unpleasant though it may seem, most dogs, and certainly all puppies, are infected with round- and tapeworms. Roundworms are more common than tapeworms and you may rest assured your puppy will have been born with an infestation of the revolting thin, white worms. Check with the breeder whether the puppy has been wormed and inform your vet accordingly. Tapeworms are flatter than roundworms and will probably be seen in the dog's faeces, so keep a check. It is best to treat the dog on a regular basis.

Opposite *A dog will tend to be more headstrong than a bitch.*

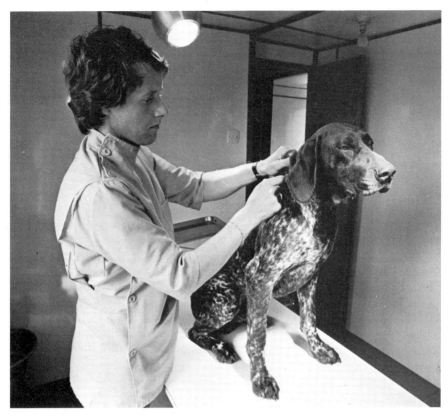

*Rely implicitly on the advice of your vet.*

When you collect the puppy, be prepared for the worst! Taken from the warmth and comfort of familiar surroundings, less than three months old, you may confidently expect it to dribble, be sick and defecate on the journey home. Your best course is to line a cardboard box with newspaper and harden your ears and heart to the plaintive whimpers. I can only recall one puppy which gave me no trouble and that was a German shorthaired pointer. The journey was some 200 plus miles by car, but the little fellow just snuggled down on an old coat and went to sleep.

# 4  A question of kennels

Before bringing your puppy home, you will doubtless have discussed with your family and come to a decision on whether it is to be kennelled out-of-doors or kept in the house. There is no doubt that a working gundog should be kennelled outside. You may find it more agreeable to have your companion in the house, sitting by your desk or relaxing in front of a roaring fire as you reflect on the day's sport, but you are choosing to please yourself and in so doing you will soften the animal. A kennelled dog will feel secure and happy in the knowledge that it has its own 'home', and will also be far easier to manage. In addition, a dog that lives out-of-doors in a variety of weather will be harder and more healthy than one which becomes used to central heating and the comforts of domesticity. Of course, you do not have to ban the dog from the house. You can operate a system of outdoor kennel and permission to come into the house for brief periods.

Having said that, let's be quite clear on one thing. The kennel must provide a dry, warm shelter and it must be kept clean and hygienic. An ideal kennel will have a wooden shelter, and if there is only one dog it need not be too large. The shelter should have two doors, if that is practical: one, facing the run and with a sliding shutter, for the dog; and the other, on the outside, to enable you to clean the kennel. There should be a wooden board raised off the floor, on which the dog can sleep. Do not, under any circumstances, give the animal straw to sleep on. It will have to be changed often, and may also encourage skin irritation or even vermin. Some owners provide no floor covering and, although this may appear spartan, dogs kept under these circumstances do very well. A good answer is to use a pile of sacks, which again must be changed whenever they become too grubby.

If you do choose to keep the dog in the house, it must have its own basket. Do not obtain one immediately, but wait until the puppy is five or six months old. As a small puppy, it will spend hours exercising its teeth on the basket until it is virtually destroyed. Far better to provide a wooden box with a blanket.

Do not put a young puppy outside for the first few weeks. Remember it has just been removed from the snug warmth and comfort of its dam and litter brothers and sisters. You may have two or three nights disturbance as the puppy protests its loneliness, but at least it should be warm and gain confidence through the knowledge that human comfort is close at hand. This is the time when house training can also be taught. Expect a few puddles and messes,

*A dog kennelled out of doors will be hardy and fit.*

but whenever you find one give the puppy a sharp, reproving 'no' and take it outside for a few moments. The real art of house training is anticipation; in other words, give the youngster the opportunity to empty itself at regular intervals outside.

The transference to the outside kennel can be done gradually. You will obviously have constructed a run. This should be long and narrow, and made of concrete, with a surround of breeze blocks to a height of nearly 60 cm (2 ft), to keep out draughts, topped with really strong wire netting. Some dogs quickly become escape artists chewing, digging and biting their way out of even the most apparently dog-proof pen. There should also be a gate in the run. Instead of breeze blocks, you can use wooden boards, which should be continued along the bottom of the gate. The run must be cleaned out daily and any remains of bones cleared away.

The puppy can be put into the run during the day and will quickly come to prefer its new home. Choose a warm night, harden your heart and put the pup out for good. Both of you will be grateful in the long run.

If you are a handyman, or have a tame carpenter available, you will obviously be able to build a kennel and run yourself. However, you can purchase ready-made kennels, which usually come in sections and are relatively easy to erect.

If you have the space, a grass run or paddock is a considerable boon for a puppy. It can self-exercise and work off surplus energy that might otherwise be put to destructive use. However, such a run will at once present a challenge to escape; make certain that the wire is dug in round the perimeter. The ground should also be well drained, otherwise it will revert to a smelly morass.

As far as general hygiene is concerned, the kennel will need to be disinfected at regular intervals, otherwise you risk a build-up of parasites. In the summer, dogs are likely to pick up ticks and fleas; this is especially so with long-haired dogs, and once an infestation is discovered it must be treated ruthlessly. Destroy all bedding and scrub the kennel with a powerful disinfectant, making sure that corners and cracks receive attention, for it is here that fleas breed and they are difficult to eradicate once established. The dog itself will require several attacks with a veterinary spray following a bath. Spray at least four times a week and examine the dog regularly, parting the hair along the chest and belly and under the legs. A thin-skinned dog, such as a pointer, will present few problems, a good bath usually being sufficient to rid it of the vermin.

41

Some summers seem to be worse than others, and one can be fighting a constant battle against skin vermin. Always pay attention if you see the dog scratching persistently.

Spaniels require careful grooming as their long coats, feathers and, in particular, their ears gather burrs and thorns. However long it takes, every burr must be removed, which can be a lengthy and tedious business, for both the owner and the dog. If left round the ears, hard, matted lumps of hair will tangle round the obstructions, until eventually they (not the ears!) have to be cut away.

All dogs should be groomed and brushed regularly, and their general health constantly monitored.

# 5 Feeding

Every writer on dogs seems to have his own pet feeding theories—I am no exception. However, one virtue I would claim for my particular method is simplicity. Dogs are carnivorous animals with jaws and digestive systems designed to cope with chunks of raw meat. In the wild state, the dog would tear freshly-killed flesh from its victim, swallowing unchewed portions as swiftly as possible in the competition to secure protein, before its pack fellows or some other wild beast deprived it of its share. Today's dog is no different. My only close acquaintance with 'lap dogs' is a pekinese, and I have noted his belligerence, courage and system of life which, in nearly all respects, is similar to the gundogs which live outside and work for their living.

For some reason, many new owners regard the feeding of a dog as an uncharted sea of troubles. How many meals? How much meat? Should he feed biscuits alone or bones—if so what sort of bones? Fish, eggs, milk, scraps . . . the list is endless. Yet the entire problem, if problem it is, can be distilled into two simple words: meat and biscuits. Until recently, I invariably fed the dogs on raw meat. Paunches, containing the vegetable contents, are ideal and dogs thrive on them. However, it is now extremely difficult to obtain raw flesh and a substitute has to be made. Although vets may tell you the opposite, I believe that raw meat is better than cooked meat for a dog. For this reason, I feed tubes of a minced offal obtained from the butcher at a fraction of the cost of tinned meats. This, mixed with a dry food substitute, provides a really nourishing meal for any dog.

There are a number of dry food substitutes which can be fed in pelleted form, and which require no additional meat, though water must always be available. They are clean to handle, appear to be found palatable, and dogs that are fed solely on them certainly seem

43

to thrive. They are used extensively in professional kennels where economy, time and cleanliness are important factors.

Nevertheless, having said that, I still make sure that my gundog has raw meat in some form in its diet. One has only to visit a foxhounds' kennels to realize that meat, fed in its natural state, is the best diet for a working dog. A hound may have to cover twenty or more miles in a day, perhaps twice a week; the kennel huntsman will have his charges in peak fitness, ready to run all day long solely on a diet of flesh.

Bones are important in a dog's diet, but there are bones and bones. Do not give Fido cooked bones of any sort. All the goodness has been extracted from them so that the dog is left with a splintery, useless relic which, if it eats it, may cause digestive trouble. Avoid chicken bones like the plague, because they can break into dagger-like splinters, perhaps perforating a bowel lining. A friend lost a spaniel through this very cause, the dog dying in agony. If you offer a raw, meaty bone, a large, chunky beef bone from the butcher, the type that a dog can happily exercise its teeth and patience on for hours on end, that is a very different matter. By sheer persistence and hard work, your dog will eventually break up the largest bone, and that is the time to remove the splinters, before he swallows one.

As far as liquid is concerned, make sure the dog always has access to water ... clean water! If he lives in an outside kennel, his bowl must be refilled and cleaned every day when the run is inspected. And of course let him have a drink on a working day at midday, and at the end of the shoot. If you cannot guarantee clean water on the shoot, carry some in a plastic container together with his bowl. Milk is excellent for puppies and growing youngsters, but it is unnecessary for an adult dog; it can cause diarrhoea, and it may contribute to excess weight, which is particularly undesirable in a gundog. Labradors and elderly spaniels seem prone to weight problems and adult fat, once laid down, is singularly difficult to remove. A bitch that has been spayed will need to have her diet closely watched, in order to make sure that she does not become obese. By the same token, never feed titbits between meals or any fattening foods. A dog that begs for scraps from the table is a nuisance and should swiftly be taught the error of its ways.

When should an adult dog be fed? Gundogs, in or out of work,

Opposite *Feeding time should present no problems.*

44

thrive on one meal a day, given in the early evening. If the dog has had a really tough day's work, let him settle in his kennel for at least half-an-hour before offering him his meal, but make sure that he has the opportunity to drink his fill.

Do not worry if your dog is a fussy feeder; some animals will bolt their food greedily, others will toy and play with it, but providing there is nothing physically wrong with the animal, it will eat exactly the amount it requires. Some working gundogs appear to exist on starvation rations despite all that their owners do to make them consume more. Obviously if your dog normally eats up well and is suddenly 'off' its food, you must consider the possibility of illness, and act accordingly.

Puppies must be treated like children; little and often is the motto. Up to three months of age the puppy will need four meals a day, reducing to three meals up to five months, and two meals at eight to nine months, when the dog can be switched to one meal a day. The four puppy meals should consist of a breakfast of finely chopped mince mixed with warm milk and crumbled puppy biscuit; midday and afternoon meals of milk and some form of porridge or Farex; and an evening meal similar to the first one. Do not overfeed the puppy, but use your common sense; if it is leaving food you are probably giving it too much, so alter the rations accordingly.

Find out what the optimum weight of your breed of dog should be, and see how closely your particular specimen accords; if you want to weigh your dog simply weigh yourself, then yourself holding the dog, and deduct your weight from the total of dog plus yourself.

# 6  Basic training

Dogs, like horses and humans, vary in their attitudes to work and their ability to absorb and retain instruction. They also have a wide range of intellect; there are bright dogs, run-of-the-mill dogs, and stupid dogs. Occasionally, and only very occasionally, one comes across a genuinely vicious dog, an unfortunate which has been born thus. It is the owner who is responsible for the behaviour of his or her dog. If it refuses to obey the simple, basic commands, such as walking quietly to heel, returning when it is called and staying when it is told to, that is a reflection on the owner, who has failed to ensure that the dog knows what it is supposed to do.

Provided that you have acquired a dog of the right temperament, from the correct stable, and that you are conversant with its limitations and understand the extent of its duties, then by a slow, careful process of training, calling for the exercise of elementary common sense on your part, there is every likelihood that you will form a satisfactory working partnership.

Is there a secret to training a dog? If there is, it is quite simply that one must make every effort to understand the dog's point of view, to think, if you like, as a dog does. You must appreciate that you are dealing with an animal of limited intelligence, an animal that wishes to please, that can understand your commands and moods from the tone of your voice, but which, like a child, is easily distracted and unable to concentrate for long periods. The redoubtable Barbara Woodhouse does not, as she would probably be the first to admit, possess some strange and secret power over animals. What she does have, however, is an empathy towards dogs and a pronounced streak of common sense.

Today gundogs are trained with a mixture of kindness, sense and firmness. In the past, the training of a dog for the field was known as breaking. The animal's spirit was broken and faults were beaten out of it. No effort was made to understand the dog's point of view. It was, of course, a more harsh and perhaps a more practical era, when dogs that did not make the grade would be discarded.

Early training can commence when the puppy is about three months old. This will not be the strict teaching of later months, but a mixture of playing and coaxing so that the puppy scarcely realizes it is being taught but absorbs, almost unconsciously, certain basic elements of its education. Play gently with the puppy and gain its confidence; at that early age you will be imprinting your personality on the little creature; so much so, that it will come to understand that its entire life revolves around you. You are the central pivot of its existence.

The first element of training is to teach the puppy its name. Use it at every opportunity, and particularly at meal-times, so that it will come to associate its name with the pleasure of being fed. But what to call it? Keep to one syllable; the best name is one that can be barked out as a sharp command, a name such as Pip, Sam or Jet.

A dog can have only one master or mistress. It is so important in these early, formative weeks and months that the puppy under- stands to whom it is responsible, and it is worth emphasizing again the importance of ensuring that your family appreciates that the new addition is not a plaything or a pet; it has been acquired for a specific purpose and must be taught its role in life. Of course, the puppy should be played with and made a fuss of. In fact, it is vital that it should be 'humanized', and exposed to everyday facets of normal life, but, when the time comes for lessons, it must understand that it is answerable only to the person who will ultimately handle it.

## The 'hup'
The puppy will swiftly react to its name, provided it is repeated sufficiently often, and at meal-times. Next, it must be taught to sit on command. This can be achieved, quickly and with a minimum of fuss, again at meal-times, using the word 'hup'. This is a shortening of the command 'hold up', a relic of the muzzle-loading days when dogs were expected to sit after a shot as fowling-pieces were recharged. At each meal-time, make the puppy sit in front of its bowl by gently pressing on its hindquarters and at the same time repeat- ing the order. Let it eat only when the command has been executed correctly, and within a surprisingly short time the youngster will sit automatically as the command is snapped out.

The 'hup' with hand signal.

It is imperative that this early lesson is mastered perfectly, for it is the basis of all future work. When you deliver the command hold up your right hand, palm down, and soon the puppy will associate dropping with the simple action of raising your arm to this position. The command 'hup' can, at a later stage, be abbreviated to a hiss. Curiously dogs seem to acknowledge a sibilant hiss with just as much energy as they do a louder order, and the hiss has the advantage of being quieter in the field. It is also surprising just how far the sound carries; certainly to at least 100 metres (100 yd) on a quiet day.

At this point, let us deal with the controversial question of correction, or punishment. In the bad old days of dog breaking, the whip was applied without hesitation and was considered a necessary adjunct of breaking or training. Today, trainers adopt a more humane and demonstrably effective means of instilling the rudiments of education. However, punishment must on occasion be administered, particularly if a dog is wilfully disobedient. The lesson must be short, sharp and it must be handed out so that the animal is quite clear in its own mind why it is being punished.

Remember that a dog is a pack animal, and being a member of your family in no way lessens that instinct. There is a pecking order in nearly all forms of life, and your puppy will soon realize its place. When punishing it, a thorough shaking by the throat will be far more effective than beating it; this is the instinctive action of a dominant dog, to go for the throat. Hold the dog by the loose skin of the throat with both hands and growl at it fiercely.

The dog must be punished in the act of committing a crime. If, for example, it runs in having been told to sit, it is quite pointless to punish it should it return; it will at once associate the punishment with having come back to you *at your request*. You will simply have to run after the dog while it is still disobeying you; by threatening it when it returns, you merely create total confusion in its mind.

All this, when you think about it, is fairly obvious and straightforward; simply a question of seeing things from the youngster's point of view. This brings us to a few basic facts of training, facts to which *you* must adhere.

In the first place, lessons must be short, initially no more than ten minutes at a time, and they must be looked on by the puppy as a privilege. Secondly, never attempt to impart a lesson if you are feeling out of sorts, grumpy, or have had a bad day at the office. You will be short-tempered, and the first hint of a mistake on the part of your pupil will generate a reaction out of all proportion to the

*Punishment must be meted out while the dog is committing a crime.*

*Teaching the dog to walk to heel.*

misdeed. The dog will immediately sense your mood and act accordingly. You must be serene, and you must want to enjoy the training session. In this frame of mind you will be able to accept mistakes and errors and forgive or punish with justice.

## Walking to heel

In these very early days, when the puppy is still under six months, it is wise to teach it to walk quietly to heel both on and off a lead. The introduction to the lead can be an occasion fraught with drama. The youngster, hitherto relatively unshackled, suddenly finds its neck constricted and its forward movement confined. The result is likely to be a frantic plunging and scrabbling which may end in near hysteria. All this can be avoided by common sense.

Firstly, use a light so-called choke chain, which relaxes as the dog ceases to strain forward. Do not just clip on a leather collar, attach a lead and hope for the best. Far better to put on a lightweight collar a few days before you intend to use the choke chain, so that the animal becomes used to an attachment round its neck.

If you are right-handed always teach the dog to walk at heel on your left side so that it will not be in the way of the gun when it is carried under your arm. Be very calm, and quiet when you attach the choke collar and lead, patting and reassuring the dog. Carry a light cane in your right hand, but do not wave it about in a threatening manner. The ideal you are aiming for is that the young dog should walk quietly at your heel, stopping when you stop and never poking its nose ahead of you. The command to use is 'heel'. Hold the end of the lead and the cane in your right hand, with the left hand grasping the lead slightly in front and to the side of your left thigh. Walk forward, and as the dog lunges ahead tap it lightly on the nose and say 'heel', firmly and sharply. Do not keep the dog on the lead for more than a few minutes; if bright, it will quickly come to understand what you are aiming at. Do try to make sure that you achieve a good walk to heel as few things are more annoying or distracting when you are shooting than a dog that is persistently edging forward, and constantly has to be checked.

At this stage of training you will, assuming sensitivity and awareness on your part, swiftly come to evaluate the puppy's approach to life; a bold, headstrong dog will probably accept the choke chain but lunge forward, irritated at this sudden restriction to its freedom; while a shy, retiring youngster may be totally inhibited, squatting in frozen panic as you try to encourage it forward. If this last is the case, simply remove the lead and forget the lesson for that day. Hasten slowly must ever be your motto and by dint of perseverance and encouragement, coupled with the ability to make the young dog feel secure, you will achieve your goal. If you simply reduce your efforts to dragging the puppy on the lead—and this is often seen—you will merely encourage resistance.

You may, of course, strike lucky, and find that the dog quickly assimilates the lesson, walking quietly at your side to the command 'heel' within a lesson or two. So much depends on the animal's temperament and your own approach.

Remember that each lesson must be fully absorbed, totally understood and correctly carried out before moving on to the next one. The cardinal sin of the novice trainer is to hurry through the, to him, rather boring elements of basic training in order to advance to the more spectacular business of retrieving and hunting. To astonish one's friends with an apparently precocious six-month-old puppy which can do everything, including play the piano, is all too often the beginner's sole aim.

At this stage in the proceedings, it is hoped, in fact assumed, that the young dog is now living out of doors in its own kennel and run. It is more than probable that you may be able to give it only one major exercise a day, having let it run for a few minutes in the early morning to empty itself. It will now welcome its combined exercise and training session with extra zest, a vigour that might well be lacking were it to be mooning round the house all day, getting under everyone's feet and into bad habits.

Do not forget to keep your actual training period short and hopefully sweet, but you must, naturally, let the dog have a good run beforehand to expel surplus energy.

### The drop

Once walking to heel has been mastered successfully, the next stage, and indeed the keystone of the entire training programme, is to teach the drop; from this so many other good things cometh! You have already taught the puppy to sit before allowing it to gulp its meal, using the command 'hup', and now we merely extend this, incorporating it into the walk at heel. Our ultimate goal is to be able to drop the dog on command or whistle at any distance and, eventually, to see the dog dropping of its own accord to flush or ground game. This latter will apply more particularly to spaniels or HPRs working cover; even if the dog does not actually sit or drop, it should

*Teaching the drop with the dog working to heel.*

stop of its own accord. Failure to instil this lesson correctly will result in birds, rabbits and hares being chased; the last thing one wants in a gundog.

Let us try to teach the dog to drop correctly. To start with, when it is walking to heel, one can give the 'hup' command, making sure that every time you do so the dog sits; let it stay in this position for a few seconds before giving the command 'walk on'. At this stage, it is best not to use the whistle, as it may confuse the juvenile mind. It is advisable to keep the whistle for the part of the programme when the dog is free of restraint. Do not forget to raise your hand, with the palm down, as you give the 'hup' order.

Let us assess what we hope to have achieved by now. The dog knows and answers to its name; it walks quietly to heel; it sits and stays by your side on command. If this is so, it is time to incorporate the use of a whistle, for the next lesson is to teach the puppy to sit on command at ever increasing distances from you, and to return to you on command and whistle.

## Whistle-wise

As far as the actual type of whistle is concerned, most trainers choose two; one should be high-pitched and penetrating, the other a loud, pea-whistle which carries an ear-splitting blast. The latter will be used only in emergencies. Both whistles should be plastic, and can be carried on a cord round one's neck. A useful refinement is a thumb-stick incorporating two whistles, each of a different pitch, in the Y-shaped head of the stick.

Simplicity and restraint are the watchwords where the whistle is concerned. An orchestration of blasts, toots and squeaks from a red-faced and increasingly frantic handler is an all too common sight at tests and trials. Your range of whistle signals should be kept brief and to the point—only blow it when you really mean to convey a message! Too often the whistle becomes, in the mouth of the nervous novice trainer, a form of moral support—the louder and more frequently he or she blows it, the greater the salve to the conscience when all goes awry.

For the sit or hup, all you require is a single sharp note; nothing more, nothing less. You can teach this simple signal to the dog when it is walking to heel by simply dropping the animal with upraised hand; a slight jerk on the lead is necessary, and a single note. Once the dog has grasped the message, it can be 'hupped' a few metres from you, again using the whistle and, assuming all goes well, at

Right *The drop at a distance.*

Below *Recalling the dog from a distant drop.*

ever increasing distances. Vary the routine. Drop the dog by your side and then walk away, first a few metres, until you can safely retreat 100 or more metres without turning your back, and are confident that the dog will stay without budging. If it moves forward, and it almost certainly will to start with, you must walk back to the dog and take it back to the spot where it was originally dropped, emphasizing the drop command with a single note on the whistle.

Initially you may find that you can walk backwards only a short distance, but keep firm control over the dog with your hand upraised and ready to drop him, and blow the whistle at the first sign of restless movement.

Once the animal has this lesson firmly implanted in its brain, you can take the lesson a stage further by calling the dog in from the drop. Do this with a series of short peeps on the whistle. The dog will rush to you, but do not let it jump or attempt to slobber you. As it reaches your feet, drop it again with hand and whistle signal, so that it sits at your feet until released.

Make it stay in this position for thirty or more seconds, then retreat a few paces and again whistle it into you with a drop at your feet. If you can achieve this in two or three short lessons you can feel well satisfied. Obviously there will be individual problems, but given patience and understanding, there is no reason why any gundog, of whatever breed, should not be capable of reaching this elementary standard.

The three divisions of gundog that we are considering – retrievers, spaniels and HPRs—all require this basic training, irrespective of the roles they are intended for in adult life. And it is worth emphasizing again that no advance in the training programme should be considered until you are quite satisfied that the dog fully understands each individual component covered so far.

# 7  The retrieve

Now we can move on to the retrieve, that part of the training programme which the novice trainer finds so satisfying and which, so
often, he rushes. That is not to say that from the earliest days the
instinct to pick up and carry should be stifled. The puppy will
happily retrieve a knotted handkerchief thrown a short distance; do
not worry if it runs off with it to its basket, or a corner, for a quick,
comforting chew. If you can encourage it to come to you, well and
good. Then, gently and with care, you can remove the handkerchief
from its mouth and give it a rewarding pat. Never, ever drag an object
from the dog's mouth, either roughly or in anger. The puppy may
have picked up your favourite slippers or gloves, but remember that
they are tainted with your scent, and it is merely pursuing its
instinct to retrieve. A dog kept in the house can swiftly run into
trouble at this point; members of the family have certain valued
possessions which, understandably, they prefer to remain unchewed and dribbled on. As a result, an article may be snatched from
the dog's mouth amidst expressions of anger, so that the unfortunate
animal swiftly becomes confused. On the one hand, its trainer
appears to require it to pick up objects and carry them in its mouth,
but it receives abuse for doing just that under certain circumstances.

**Dummies**
As far as dummies are concerned, the initial training dummies can
be made from plastic containers, such as washing-up liquid bottles,
filled with sand to give weight and wrapped in sacking. Do not, at
this stage, use dummies made from rabbit or hare skins, or with
dried wings attached to them, as the young dog may be tempted to
chew them. Alternatively, you can make a small dummy from two or
three old socks rolled up together.

Do not, under any circumstances, introduce gunfire at this stage; that is a gradual process, which, if it is rushed or undertaken too soon, can all too easily leave you with a gun-nervy dog. We will move on to that subject shortly, but first, you must get the youngster retrieving the dummy straight back to you, happily and efficiently. You do not want a dog that dashes out without a by-your-leave when the dummy is thrown, sniffs the dummy, picks it up in its teeth, tosses it in the air and then, as a final indignity, rolls on it! Nor do you want a dog which picks the dummy and returns to the handler, then circles round the trainer, coyly and bloodymindedly making it quite clear that it has not the slightest intention of having this delicious plaything removed, instead of delivering the object to hand. Least of all do you want a dog that potters out to the fall, takes a perfunctory sniff at the dummy, and then wanders off on some obscure business of its own.

Although you can convey a feeling of pleasure and play to the dog on the occasion of its first retrieving lesson, from your point of view this is a crucial time and there can be no allowance for sloppiness on your part or that of the dog. There are one or two points worth noting. As usual, keep the lessons short and sweet and, as always, end on a successful note. If you terminate a lesson abruptly, having scolded the dog for failing to follow your directions, it will remember the unpleasantness at the start of the next day's lesson.

Quite often, a dog returns to its trainer in a hesitant fashion or sidles off in another direction because the handler stands tall and fixes his whole gaze and attention on the animal. A dog has a very different outlook on life. His viewpoint is perhaps only 50–60 cm (20–24 in) off the ground, and to him you will appear awe-inspiringly high. Animals loathe being stared at. A cat or a dog will quickly avert its eyes if you gaze steadily at it so, when the dog starts to return with the dummy, crouch down on your heels and try to avoid looking directly into its eyes.

The first throw of the dummy should be on clean ground, a lawn is quite adequate; tall grasses and bushes are for later work, when the dog can be taught to mark the thrown dummy and use its nose. At this stage, all that is needed is a clean pick-up and return to hand.

Sit the youngster by your side, and let it sniff the dummy, then throw it fifteen or so metres. Do not worry if the dog dashes after it as soon as it hits the ground, but give the command 'go fetch' as it does so. As the dog picks up the dummy, start to move backwards quite fast, encouraging the dog in with your hands and giving the return

Left *The dog is told to stay while the dummy is thrown.* Right *The dog is sent out.* Below *The trainer crouches to encourage the dog to return to him with the dummy.*

command on the whistle. The youngster will want to get back to you, and as it sees you retreating will gallop up, almost oblivious of the dummy still in its mouth. Remove the dummy gently. If the dog grips tight, as is likely to happen, insert a finger between its jaws; this will almost certainly make it release its hold. Try the entire exercise once more and then, if successful, praise the dog and make it abundantly clear that you are pleased. A short run, a walk at heel and several drops will be quite enough for this first dummy session.

The next lesson should incorporate a refinement: an essential development. You no longer want the dog to tear out for the dummy the instant you hurl it. You want it to sit to command and stay seated until given the order to fetch. At this point assistance is helpful. A dummy thrower will enable you to concentrate your attention on the dog and restrain it if necessary. As the dummy is thrown, give the command 'stay'. If the dog cannot resist the urge to spring after the dummy, restrain it with a hand across the chest. Reiterate the order with some force, allowing it to gather the dummy only after sitting for at least ten seconds. You can gradually extend the lesson, hurling the dummy to an ever-increasing distance, and keeping the dog sitting for up to a minute. Do not forget to make use of the whistle, both to drop the dog before the retrieve and at the return.

If the dog tends to drop or spit out the dummy a short distance in front of you, instead of placing it in your hand, retreat backwards as it advances on you, encouraging it all the time, and adroitly remove the dummy from its mouth as it comes up to you and before it can think of dropping it. Nothing in the field looks sloppier than a dog that spits out a bird or engages in a tug-o'-war.

A refinement to the delivery is to sit the dog as it reaches you and to make it keep the dummy in its mouth for a few seconds before you gently remove it.

Do not rush the retrieving lessons. Both of you must get this absolutely right, and if you think that the dog is becoming bored or inattentive, or is perhaps playing up after performing well, give it a rest for a day or two. Always end the lesson on a high note, so that the dog looks forward to continuing on the following day. Retrieving, indeed any lesson, should be looked on as a privilege, a reward if you like, for having stayed in its kennel most of the day.

Once you are satisfied that the dog is really enjoying retrieving and doing the task to your satisfaction, you can start to substitute dummies that give a hint of the real thing. This is the point, too, at which you can introduce gunfire.

Canvas dummies can be bought, and very useful they are too. They are weighty and have a loop at one end, which is useful for throwing. Alternatively, you can again make your own dummies. Use the same type of plastic container as before, wrap sacking around it and bind it on tightly. For a feather dummy, strap on a pair of wing feathers from a pheasant or duck, using a rubber band. Do not use wings recently cut from a bird as they will smell delicious, and the dog may be tempted to chew them, instead of bringing back the dummy. The wings should be dried from the previous season. A fur dummy can be made in much the same fashion, only this time substitute a rabbit skin for the wings. A fresh skin, with the head and feet cut off, should be salted, left for a few hours, then tightly wrapped round the sacking-covered dummy and bound in place, or held there with stout rubber bands.

## Introduction to gunfire

The way in which a young dog is introduced to gunfire is critically important. The sound of a shot can be extremely frightening to a young dog, and if you simply fire a shotgun in the animal's vicinity without prior introduction, the chances are that you will rapidly become the owner of a gun-nervy dog. The animal will flinch, look apprehensive, and, at the worst, may bolt for the nearest refuge, which will probably be its kennel. Gun-nerviness can mean that the dog becomes upset even at the sight of a gun under your arm, associating the weapon with the unpleasant fright it has received.

Gun-nerviness can be cured, but gun-shyness, all trainers agree, is quite hopeless because, probably, it is an inherited fault. At the sound of a shot, either the dog will depart at high speed with its tail between its legs to cower at a distance in extreme terror, or it may collapse on the ground in panic. There is no cure; you should either have the dog put down or find a non-shooting home for it.

If the dog does suffer from gun-nerves, as a result of an over-hasty approach to training, considerable time and patience will be required to cure it. It might be worthwhile taking the dog to a professional trainer to sort out the problem. The method some trainers use is to leave the dog completely alone for a few weeks, in order to let it recover itself and forget the upsetting experience. They then start again with basic training; and when that is once more flowing smoothly, the dog is quietly re-introduced to gunfire.

Left *Never fire the first shot close to a young dog. A starting pistol is ideal for introducing a dog to gunfire.*

Opposite *Some dogs will soon come to treat a shot with disdain.*

Of course, some dogs will take absolutely no notice of a shot, treating it with disdain, but these are exceptions. All dogs should be treated with extreme caution and consideration in this respect. Before you squeeze a trigger, make sure the dog has become accustomed to loud noises in its daily life. Bang dustbin lids when it is fed, make a clatter and general hubbub; this background noise will soon be ignored by the dog at the more exciting prospect of filling its stomach.

First gunfire should be reasonably modified, and here a small starting pistol or even a cap pistol is ideal. Again, fire the pistol while the dog is being fed and from a distance of at least 50 metres (50 yd) to start with, gradually decreasing the distance until you can fire a shot standing beside the dog. Study the animal's reactions and

Above *A dummy launcher ready for firing.*
Opposite *The dog sits while the launcher is fired.*

if, initially, it shows some degree of uneasiness, let it have a break for a day or two. Then ask a friend to fire the pistol while you stay by the dog and calm it as the gun is fired. The transition from starting pistol using blanks to ·410 shotgun, and ultimately to a 12-bore, can be taken in easy stages, depending entirely on the animal's response.

If all goes well you will now, with assistance, be in a position to advance to dummy retrieving to the sound of gunfire. A friend can throw the dummy as you fire a shot, the dog of course sitting and being released for the dummy on the command 'go fetch'.

You would be well advised to obtain a dummy launcher, one of the finest pieces of training equipment ever devised. The launcher consists of a handle attached to a hinged rim, into which a blank cartridge can be inserted and a special dummy fitted. The firing pin

is activated through the handle and the dummy can be tossed 100 metres or more into cover, water or wherever you choose. The bang together with the dummy hurling through the air at the same time, provide ideal conditions for the youngster, and also enable you to undertake this vital element of training unassisted.

Before advancing to the next stage, it is worth recapping on all that the young dog should have learnt thoroughly. It will know and answer to its name; it will sit on the command 'hup', and wait without inching forward before being released; it will walk calmly and quietly to heel on your left side without constantly having to be reminded and chivvied back; it will retrieve a feathered or furred dummy to hand on command, delivering it without fuss, and if it sits to do so, all the better; and it will have become accustomed to, and ignore, the sound of shots fired beside it.

All these individual parts of training can be combined in each session so that the dog is constantly being reminded of its duties. At this stage, you must be absolutely certain in your own mind that the dog is performing to the best of its ability and, most important of all, that it always understands what you ask it to do.

The next elements of training are: to teach the dog to drop at a distance to the sound of a shot; to work to hand signals combined with the whistle, again at a distance; to swim and enjoy water; and to jump. These routines are common to the three gundog divisions with which we are dealing: the retrievers, the spaniels and the HPRs. Their individual duties will be considered in the next chapter.

## Dropping to shot

Dropping to shot is not, as some shooting folk believe, an unnecessary training refinement; it is a vital component of the finished product, adding greatly to the spectacle of dogwork, and also, and this is more important, assisting materially with the sport. In the final analysis, a gundog is in the field to help fill the bag, by producing the quarry, retrieving it, and collecting the wounded which might otherwise be lost. A dog that drops when a shot is fired, and remains on drop, is a definite plus. The alternative is a dog which, when you fire, plunges ahead in pursuit of the bird or rabbit. Certainly, if the quarry is dead, the dog should have it in its mouth that much more swiftly; and there is a school of thought which argues that if a bird is pricked, such as a duck at evening flight when it is difficult to mark, the sooner the dog is racing after the fall or the dropping bird the better. It is an argument which does have a degree

*Teaching the drop to shot: let the dog hunt a patch of ground (left); then give the drop signal with whistle and hand, and fire the starting pistol (right).*

of validity, but unfortunately such a dog is likely to run-in at the sight of any bird coming down, including a bird belonging to another gun who is about to collect it. And nothing is more infuriating when you are rough shooting than to have a dog floundering about out of shot, putting up birds, and causing general mayhem, simply because it ran into shot instead of dropping. The extension of dropping to shot is dropping to flush, the dog either dropping or remaining still when it flushes a bird, hare or rabbit. Once you have achieved this stage you can claim to have a steady gundog. It is a state of affairs seen all too seldom on the average rough or driven shoot.

Teaching the drop to shot is relatively simple. Let the dog hunt a patch of ground, and while it is busy with its nose down, give the drop signal—a loud blast, remember — on the whistle, shout 'hup' and fire your starter pistol. The dog will quickly come to associate the sound of the shot with the signal to drop. When you are confident that the lesson has been fully absorbed you can vary the routine.

In order to emphasize the drop-to-shot command, send the dog out for a dummy, and fire a shot to drop it when it is half way there. Keep it on the drop for a few seconds and then wave it onto the fetch.

## Hand signals

Hopefully, you have now reached the stage at which the dog is alert to hand signals. A word of warning: just as the whistle command must mean something and should be used sparingly but with determination, so it is with hand signals. If you blow your whistle like a demented pixie and semaphore with your arms in all directions, it can lead only to total confusion on the part of the dog, and frustration, or a heart attack, on your part. Again, this fault is prevalent particularly among novice handlers, and is often an expression of nerves.

Hand signals must be explicit. Already, you will have used your hands as a focal point when the dog returns with a dummy by encouraging it in and patting your thighs, and also when dropping the dog with an upraised hand. One handler is so keen on making sure that his dog watches his hand signals, that he wears white gloves when running it in a test.

The intention now is to teach the dog to obey hand directions at a distance in conjunction with the whistle. Imagine a shooting situation in which a bird has been shot and dropped into a clump of rushes 100 metres away; your dog was unsighted and failed to mark the fall; perhaps it was retrieving another bird at the same time. Your object is to send it out to the fall. You will have, from a distance, to signal the dog to the fall, moving it right or left, backwards or forwards, until it scents the bird. There are few sights more pleasing in the shooting or trial field than to see an accomplished dog working with attention and care to its handler's signals from a distance.

Basic directional work can be taught with the use of two dummies. Your intention is that, when both have been thrown with the dog sitting in the 'hup' position, you will direct it to collect them in whatever order you require. Throw them as far as possible and well apart, making quite sure that the pupil does not stir. Leave the dog in position for half a minute and then, standing slightly in front of the dog so that it can see you, send it for the *first* dummy. Give the command 'go fetch' and use whichever arm is required, right or left, to indicate clearly to the dog in which direction you want it to go. It will probably set off for the last dummy to be thrown. Blow the stop whistle and if it obeys reiterate your hand command. It *may* obey, it

Hand signals must be explicit: right, left, and (overleaf) go back.

*may* set off in the required direction and retrieve the first dummy to hand. Well and good; put it on the drop again, and then send it for the last dummy. The chances are, though, that the whole exercise will fall apart and you may not be able to stop it collecting the last dummy thrown. Do not, under any circumstances, scold the dog but accept the retrieve and then start all over again. Do not try to repeat the exercise from the same spot but move on to fresh ground. It may take one, two or half-a-dozen efforts before the dog cottons on, but cotton on it will sooner or later.

This exercise is most important, incorporating several vital elements. Not only is the dog learning to watch for and obey your signals, whether hand, whistle or voice, but it is also being taught to mark the dummies and their fall. Until now, it has had to cope with a simple mental exercise, one dummy; now it is having to use its brain and develop its ability to cope with 'thinking' situations.

You have now taught the dog to move in lateral directions, right or left; and, of course, it will return to you on command. The next phase is to teach it to go away from you, to expand its area of search when hunting for a dummy or bird. This is the 'go back' command. The hand signal is simple; if you are right-handed, stand facing the dog, bring your right arm over to your left side and as you give the command, swing your arm out to point in the direction you want the dog to go.

Teaching the 'go back' is quite easy. Walk the dog to heel for 20–30 m (20–30 yd), holding a dummy in one hand; drop the dummy so that the dog sees it, walk on for a similar distance, then drop the dog and using the command and hand signal, send it back for the dummy. Gradually you can extend the distances involved until it is fetching from 100 m (100 yd).

Now you can introduce the hidden dummy. Either plant a dummy before taking the dog out, or ask a friend to assist you. The dog will not have seen the dummy but will, we trust, accept your commands and set off to search for it. Slowly and carefully, making quite sure that each lesson is absorbed, you can now use your imagination. Two dummies can be hidden to incorporate the go back and left and right signals. One dummy can be fired from a launcher and another hidden. A 'blind' retrieve can be put together by firing a dummy over the hedge into tall grass. A distraction dummy can be thrown or fired as the dog is setting off to fetch a dummy. There is a wide variety of retrieving set pieces that the handler can devise with imagination and assistance.

*Labradors, and other retrievers and spaniels, are particularly good in water.*

This groundwork must be undertaken slowly, and no phase should be missed out or rushed. If at any stage you feel the dog has not grasped a lesson then stop and go back to base one. Remember to keep the lessons short, and at intervals allow the dog a break of a day or so.

Let's recap at this point and see exactly where we have got to.

The dog answers to its name; walks to heel; drops to shot; retrieves to hand; can be directed on to a fall right or left and made to go back.

## Water

The one element we have yet to consider is water. Treated in a sensible fashion no dog will refuse to enter water; some will revel in it to the point that they cannot be kept out, while others will work in it but clearly indicate their preference for dry land. Retrievers and springers are particularly good in water, but HPRs occasionally show a dislike of the element, perhaps due to their thin skins.

*Many of the retrieving exercises using dummies can be repeated in water.*

The introduction to water should be gradual and can start in the earliest days. On no account attempt a forced entry into water. It is not unknown for people, out of frustration, to pick up a young dog and throw it into a pool or stream. However, nothing is more likely to put a dog off water for life than such stupid and brutal treatment.

I have a small stream running through a back field, a stream which in the summer is little more than tiny pools and rivulets. Here a puppy can splash happily, gradually becoming used to the element until, after a short while, it scarcely notices it. Choose a warm, sunny day for the first dip into out-of-depth water and, if possible, have with you an older dog that enjoys water work, which will give confidence to the youngster. The pool or gently-flowing stream must have a shallow edge so that the dog can gain confidence and happily splash around. Wade in yourself, encouraging the dog; throw a floating dummy into the shallows for it, and when it is retrieving this with confidence toss the dummy out a little further so that it has to paddle for it. Hasten slowly and do not worry if on the first two or three occasions you cannot get it out of its depth; if there is a genuine reluctance and nervousness you may have to move it gently and quietly into deeper water by holding and supporting it, until it feels confident. This, though, is most unusual. You will not have to teach it to swim; it will automatically paddle and though, initially, it will probably swim with its head too high, it will quickly become accomplished.

When teaching retrieving from water, remember that the dog's range of vision will be only 5–7·5 cm (2–3 in) above the water and it will, quite often, fail to see a dummy that is quite obvious to you. This is a situation where hand signals are vital; a quick peep on the whistle to catch its attention, and then a hand signal should have it swimming in the right direction. If the water is choppy the dog may only spot the dummy at the last moment, so do not become frustrated or start cursing it. Try to see things from its very low viewpoint.

Again, with water, you can repeat several of the exercises taught on land. Two dummies can be thrown and the dog sent for them in whichever order you choose. You can toss one into the water and a second on to the far bank, or you can have a dummy hidden in reeds and another in the water; the combinations are endless.

## Jumping

Like swimming, jumping is an inherent ability which gradually improves as a dog grows more experienced and develops muscle power. Jumping is probably one of the situations in the field which leads to more accidents than any other. Wire, barbed and plain, is to be avoided at all costs; ripped pads, groin and stomach tears are all too common. Do not let your dog jump wire if it can be avoided, but, of course, occasions arise when the dog is out of sight and tries to go either through or over wire; the majority of times it will get away with it, but there is always that one occasion when, through mis-judgment or haste, it may be injured. Plain wire can be equally dangerous, particularly if there are two strands over a low wall, or sheep netting. It is too easy for the dog to catch a hind leg between the wires, which twist and lock creating a trap from which there is no escape.

The best way to teach jumping is to set up two or three simple solid wooden jumps in a narrow alley or specially built run. It should not be possible for the dog to go round the edges; it must jump them if it is to reach you. By varying the height of the jumps from very low to moderate the dog will be encouraged to tackle

*A labrador, carrying a French partridge, jumps sheep-wire.*

them. Position the dog at the far end and then call it in, encouraging it with the stacatto come-in note on the whistle. Make a great fuss of the dog when it jumps them and reaches you.

Do not expect the young dog to make spectacular leaps; neither should you expect too much of it. Jumping demands a high degree of fitness, skill and courage; all of these aspects will develop, but not too soon. Some dogs become adept at surmounting obstacles, and to see a labrador flying a fence with a pheasant in its mouth is a wonderful sight.

# 8 Specialized training

So far we have dealt with basic training, and if you have achieved a satisfactory standard through the various stages you may be assured that your dog, at some twelve to sixteen months, will be ready to enter the shooting field. However, the training outlined in the previous chapters is common to the three types of gundog and, before moving on, it is necessary to consider their specialized roles.

Retrievers are the easiest with which to deal. They must walk to heel, retrieve on command and respond to commands given at a distance. Retrievers will hunt but this is not their prime task, nor is it built into their make-up; certainly they will push through cover if asked to, but they lack the drive, the zip and zest in cover of, say, an English springer. Nor will they hunt to a pattern within gunshot of the handler. Of course, there are exceptions, but this is not their intended job.

## Spaniels

A spaniel has the prime task of hunting for game in front of its handler and, when found, flushing it. However, it is essential that the dog remains within shot of the gun; a spaniel that flushes pheasants or rabbits 50 or 100 metres away is worse than useless. The dog must work a strict pattern in front of and on either side of the gun, but no more than 20 to 25 metres away; furthermore, it must drop or at least stop, when a bird is flushed or a rabbit bolts.

It is the dog that should do the work, not you. Walk in a straight line, allowing the spaniel to hunt and investigate every inch of cover within shot of you. Do not start weaving from side to side yourself as this defeats the whole object of the exercise; it is a fault commonly seen in tests, the handler being unable to accept that his dog is there to find the quarry, rather than himself.

*A spaniel's prime task is to hunt in front of the gun.*

When you are teaching quartering, you should bear in mind the direction of the wind. Normally you will work a dog into the wind so that scent is blown directly at it. This consideration is vital to working pointers, and to spaniels although many handlers probably fail to give the wind sufficient thought. If you work downwind the dog will be forced to go out further than is desirable in order to turn and hunt back to you; in doing so it may inadvertently flush game it has been unable to scent while on its way out. One should also remember that birds flushed downwind, although they will initially turn into the wind, will swiftly fly away from you.

It is pointless to try to teach a spaniel to quarter on ground that lacks any scent or interest. Ideally, you require it to bustle forward, nose to ground, and when it is approaching 20 metres from you, give a quick peep on the whistle to catch its attention and at the same time signal it to the other side; repeat the process—as the dog reaches the 20 metre mark, still hunting, attract its attention and signal it back to the first position. So you will proceed, you walking in a straight line while the dog works pendulum fashion in front. In the early stages, though, you will find that you yourself will have to zig-zag, turning the dog quickly and then moving in the opposite direction.

Choose a ground which you know is used by rabbits, but make absolutely certain before you start the lesson that every single bunny has been shifted. The last thing you require is a rabbit bolting in front of the young dog's startled eyes. If the worst should happen, give the drop signal with some force and if the dog obeys make a great fuss of him.

This is a classic situation in which punishment can be misapplied. You are teaching quartering, a rabbit bolts and the dog takes off after it while you stand, frantically blowing your whistle and shouting. Eventually the dog returns to be met by some form of punishment and evident displeasure. This is all wrong. The dog will associate the punishment with having returned to you, its last action, and not with having committed the grave fault of chasing fur.

What should you have done? Quite simply, chase after the animal yourself, drag it back to the point of flush and there express your displeasure. The punishment must be meted out while the dog is still committing the crime, otherwise it becomes quite pointless and will do more harm than good.

Most spaniels will hunt cover naturally, though some are considerably better than others. Thick, tall grass in which the youngster can happily hunt whilst you are in a position to keep a close eye on it will suffice for its introduction to cover. You must avoid entering the dog into cover that is both extensive and all-embracing, especially if there is a likelihood of game or rabbits being flushed. Summer bracken is deadly in this respect; the dog vanishes into the green jungle and at once you have lost control. Try, instead, to find small patches of bramble and thorn; if a rabbit bolts or bird flushes, drop the dog the moment it emerges from the covert, walk up to it, pat it and then make it walk to heel.

Springer spaniels are, temperamentally, the exact opposite of retrievers, and a good, energetic springer will demand a great deal of alertness from the handler; he must be 'on top' of the dog, ready at all times for a 'naughty' from that tireless bundle of energy. A top-class dog will all too swiftly recognize a trainer who allows it to get away with murder, and will take every advantage of him or her.

Retrievers and spaniels demand different temperaments from their handlers; it is often noticeable that spaniel handlers have excitable natures, being themselves full of nervous energy, while retriever owners can be more phlegmatic and calm in their outlook.

So where does that place the HPR handler?

## HPR breeds

It is important that an HPR breed is trained by its owner; more so than is the case with the other types of gundog. A strong bond of mutual understanding will be established between trainer and dog, and due to the HPR's sensitive and very 'personal' nature, the transference from trainer to owner can be fraught with problems. And besides this, very few trainers will take on HPRs.

Basic training for the HPR can be carried out exactly as previously described, but the two points to concentrate on are quartering and pointing. The latter cannot be taught, and you will probably discover that from its earliest days the pup is pointing at anything and everything from butterflies to sparrows. Discrimination will develop with maturity, though you must be prepared for some frustrating early days in the field when the young dog rigidly points skylarks and pipits.

Encourage the dog to stay on point no matter what it is; the moment it goes on point, slip on its lead, approaching it from the side, not the rear as this will lead it to think you intend it to flush. Remain with the dog and let it stay on point as long as it wishes, while you gently encourage it. You, not the dog, must then flush the quarry, dropping the dog as you do so.

It is vital that HPRs learn to drop instantly to shot, flush or bolt. I found that my own GSP quickly absorbed this lesson, going flat on its belly. Fortunately, I have many rabbits in the back field and the dog could be dropped the instant one bolted; this, coupled with a shot being fired—in the air, not at the rabbit—quickly completed the lesson.

Remember that the HPR's purpose in life is to hunt game for you, which implies working on either side of the handler up to 100 metres away, pointing it, flushing on command, marking the fall and retrieving to hand. The dog will also be expected to hunt cover.

*A GSP pointing.*

Some critics of the breeds maintain that, being thin-skinned, HPRs will not face cover, but this is absolute nonsense. Impenetrable thorns, through which a driving spaniel can push, will deter an HPR, but it can be expected to face brambles and reasonable thorn.

Do not under any circumstances rush the training of an HPR. One can enter a spaniel or retriever to the shooting field at fifteen months and expect it to carry out full duties by the end of that season, but an HPR should be treated with more caution. On no account let it retrieve wounded game in its first 'live' season; if you do, you may well end up with a hard-mouthed dog. HPRs have a reputation for this vice, although it is no more prevalent amongst them than it is amongst the other breeds; but it can break out if insufficient care is taken in those early days.

An HPR will be making far more use of its nose than, say, a spaniel or retriever, and you must make allowance for and understand this. The dog's world almost entirely revolves around scent and scenting conditions. You will quickly come to recognize whether the dog is pointing feather or fur by its attitude. Remember the wind, and the necessity to work into it whenever possible.

HPRs are also particularly useful for woodland deerstalking. Mine seemed instinctively to know what was required of it when roe stalking. He keeps slightly behind me, pauses or drops when I stop and stays still at the shot. He tracks well, using ground scent and when he finds his deer, goes straight into it and pins it. I have also found him invaluable, in thick cover, for telling me the exact whereabouts of a deer. To watch his head moving and nostrils wrinkling as he picks up the scent of a moving animal, perhaps 100 m (100 yd) away, is fascinating.

# 9 The shooting field

The introduction to the shooting field proper should be gradual; a gentle and almost unobserved transference from lessons with dummies to real, live quarry. It will demand sacrifice and control on the part of the handler, who must not, under any circumstances, carry a gun. To do so is fatal. One cannot shoot over a young, totally inexperienced dog and expect both to slay one's quarry with anything approaching skill, and to concentrate on restraining those hitherto dormant passions inflamed by the sight and sound of pheasants flushing or rabbits bolting.

Before letting the young dog see warm game, it should have a series of retrieves with cold game. If you can obtain them, use mallard or wigeon for the first attempts as their feathers are short and less likely to clog the dog's mouth. A pheasant or partridge, clumsily picked up, may drop to the ground leaving the youngster with nothing but feathers and possibly a strip of skin. Pigeon should at this stage be avoided at all costs; their feathers are so loosely attached that they fall out in mouthfuls. There is no reason why a cold, dead rabbit should not be used, but be careful that, whether a duck or rabbit, it is cleanly shot. A gaping wound is only likely to arouse the dog's curiosity. Let the dog sniff the bird or rabbit in your hands, make it sit and then throw the game a short distance. Hold the dog up until it is desperate to retrieve, then send it out and encourage it back so that it has picked and brought the game to hand before it has had time to question it.

The first few days in the live shooting field must be spent with a

Opposite *Let the dog sniff cold game before it is allowed to retrieve warm game.*

friend—preferably a good shot—who will do all the shooting. You will be controlling the dog and only allowing it to retrieve simple, stone-dead birds; if it is a spaniel, a few short hunts can be allowed but only in a situation where there is no chance of it getting out of control.

Your chief hazard in these early, tentative days will be the danger of the dog running-in to either flush or shot. It is a fault that must be stamped on immediately. It indicates that the dog is not secure in this vital aspect of its training, and you will have to call a halt to current activities and return to the basic training ground. Do not even contemplate any extension of the real thing if you have a question mark over any aspect of the training programme.

Assuming that all goes well on this first outing, an outing which should be kept short and in an area where you can almost guarantee one or two retrieves and the odd temptation but not a surfeit of game, let there be a pause of at least a week before the next foray, a week which can be filled with attention to basic training.

The introduction to the shooting field in that first season should consist of a series of stage-managed productions, each providing the youngster with further experience and opportunities to widen its mental and physical abilities. Take it slowly and quietly, foregoing the gun for as long as possible. The ideal course of action would be to handle the young dog in that first season, without recourse to carrying a shotgun yourself.

In the early days do try to avoid contact with other dogs. They may be more experienced, they will certainly be jealous and they can undo the work of months in a few moments. The last thing you require is an older dog running-in and trying to snatch a retrieve from your dog. A tug-o'-war will result which the youngster will probably lose; even worse is the sight of an ill-trained dog tearing after a rabbit or pheasant. Suddenly your hitherto impeccable young dog may start to acquire some rather nasty ideas. Dogs that whine, dogs that bite their game, dogs that are constantly shouted at or beaten by their owners, dogs that run round the shooting field creating mayhem—such as these and their wretched owners, are to be avoided at all costs. One even comes across the occasional gun-dog owner who thinks it amusing to have an ill-mannered dog. It is not. It is merely ignorance on his part that calls for condemnation, and sadness on behalf of the dog, which knows no better.

Water work should also be introduced gradually. A flight pond at dusk can present a variety of hazards and once the youngster has vanished into the dark it may consider that the ties of obedience are temporarily in abeyance. Water is important and if you can arrange for it to retrieve one or two easy duck in daylight so much the better. This is where the wildfowler's dog, working under isolated conditions, close to its master and with little extraneous temptation, scores. Likewise the pigeon shooter using his dog from a hide will be in a position to control the situation rather more readily than the shooter who has the dog working at a distance. Of course, both fowling on the shore and pigeon shooting call for special attributes on the part of the dog. Wildfowling invariably raises the hoary old chestnut: is it not better for a dog to run-in at night and, by its swift reaction, pick a duck, perhaps pricked, which may be lost to a dog that waits to be given the order to fetch? There is much common sense in such an attitude but, regrettably, this type of discrepancy is difficult to confine to a particular situation; it tends to become a habit. Dogs used a great deal for duck shooting quickly learn how to deal with pricked birds, which have a habit of diving and swimming underwater. However, such wisdom only comes with experience and to see a young dog grab a mouthful of water as a duck vanishes below the surface is highly comical.

Without doubt, the major hazard to the young dog in the field is ground game. A rabbit or hare bolting from beneath the dog's nose presents an almost irresistible temptation as it streaks away, white scut bobbing tantalizingly. The very movement of the creature will trigger a reaction unless discipline has been drilled home. I dislike intensely the use of check cords in the field for I am quite convinced that the dog is well aware of the cord's presence and what it implies but will revert to its former evil ways once it is removed.

This is where the use of a training-pen scores hands down. The pen consists of an enclosure in which are kept a dozen or so rabbits or young pheasants. Unfortunately it is not the type of equipment that is readily available to the novice trainer, although he might be fortunate enough to come across a professional who will let him use his pen. The young dog can be taught, within the confines of its wire perimeter, the truths concerning, in particular, rabbits. Bunnies will bolt from piles of brush, and the dog can be stopped from chase at once, being dropped on the whistle and 'hup' signal. Bear in mind, however, that too much use of the training-pen will breed familiarity in the dog, who will quickly wise-up to the situation.

At the end of the day, the best training with fur is under battle conditions, but with the handler fully alert and aware that rabbits or

Above *A labrador learns steadiness in a pheasant rearing-pen.*
Opposite *Picking-up is a sport in its own right.*

hares are likely to pop up at any minute. It all comes back to that vital drop signal and the dog's response. Quite often you will spot a rabbit or hare before the dog does; walk up quietly, ready to let loose all hell if the dog fails to drop the instant the fur bolts.

If all goes well, shoot a rabbit or two but make sure they are stone-dead before the dog is allowed to fetch. An old buck or doe, with plenty of life left in it, can give a hesitant youngster a nasty time and even induce hard mouth as it squeezes the rabbit in irritation. On a similar note, never let a young dog pick up grey squirrels. When injured, they can inflict a very unpleasant bite.

Some gundog writers suggest that picking-up is a useful means of teaching a young dog its trade. I could not disagree more! A day's driven shooting is not the correct place in which to give a youngster its final polish. It is fair neither to the keeper, the guns nor the dog.

The keeper requires pickers-up who know their business and are not going to waste time fiddling about with dogs which could, quite possibly, cause a major upset in the programme.

For a young dog the excitement and temptations at a formal day's shoot could prove disastrous; it may see ill-mannered dogs belonging to the guns, dogs which whine at their masters' pegs during a drive and then sloppily retrieve birds lying dead in the open a few yards from the gun. There is invariably, too, the hazard of wounded birds, known as runners, which have to be collected. Frequently these will fall into the next drive and the keeper may issue instructions that birds are to be picked only from the first 20 metres of that covert, other birds to be gathered after that drive. A young dog may choose to ignore your whistle and quite possibly go almost berserk as it finds itself surrounded by pheasants, fluttering up in delicious and tempting flurries. It is a situation which can scarcely be contemplated; it will lead to the immediate expulsion of the handler from the shoot, and will probably destroy weeks of training in a few minutes.

Once your dog has become accustomed to the shooting field, with only one gun and a handler accompanying it and it is felt that it can now broaden its experience, one can approach a keeper and, explaining the situation to him, ask whether it would be feasible to bring the young dog along for one or two shoots purely as an observer. If he agrees, spend a morning, no more, at the shoot, and station yourself behind guns who lack dogs. Explain to the gun and the nearest picker-up what you are about so that neither expect you to deal with the slain. Then, and only then, and subject to the keeper's agreement, is it time to consider allowing the dog to pick up. Remember that you are there on sufferance at this stage and a close eye will be kept on both of you. Do not try any fancy retrieves or overstretch the dog in order to show off. Both of you will doubtless come to grief.

Once you are accepted, picking-up can become a sport in itself; good pickers-up are greatly in demand, to the extent that some people set aside their guns and concentrate solely on the pleasures of dog handling, aware that they are performing a useful and humane task.

# 10 Somewhere to shoot

At this point you should be in possession of a well-trained, useful gundog; a dog which would be accepted in all normal gundog circles without causing either of you embarrassment. Where, though, are you going to use your companion? You may, of course, already have access to rough shooting, driven game, wildfowling or pigeon shooting. If so, well and good; there is no problem.

For many people, however, any kind of shooting is difficult to obtain, and, owing to the sport's increasing popularity, the number of shoots and areas available for exploitation are diminishing each year. Nevertheless, having said that, shooting can still be found and though your rent is likely to be considerably more than the pre-war bottle of whisky for 500 acres of rough shooting, it can still be acquired within the compass of most pockets.

The lines of approach are straightforward. If your purse is sufficiently well lined, you should have little trouble finding what you require through the classified columns of the shooting magazines. You may wish to rent a small shoot solely for yourself or you may form a small syndicate of like-minded friends, each prepared to pay his subscription and help out on the shoot itself. Rough shoots of this nature, perhaps 500 to 1,500 acres, can be enormous fun and, depending on their location, offer a wide variety of sport, including pigeon and duck shooting and ferreting, quite apart from walked-up game. DIY shoots are becoming increasingly popular and offer the dogman considerable scope for his charge. On such a shoot a gundog will quickly learn to deal with a wide variety of situations and become shoot-wise.

Modest rough shooting, pigeoning and rabbiting, can still be found, though it would be foolish to pretend that it is easy to obtain, unless one lives right off the beaten track. The only answer is to make contacts, to get to know local keepers and estate managers. By offering to beat on estates in the shooting season, you will quickly discover what shooting is like at the blunt end and may also obtain invitations to end-of-season cock shoots and vermin and pigeon shoots. From such small beginnings great things can often spring but it takes hard work, intelligence and the right and willing approach. The knowledge that you have a good dog may often stand you in good stead, but beware of using your young dog in the beating line. This is a certain road to ruination. On either side there will be dogs of varying ability, under varying degrees of control. In thick cover you may well lose sight and sound of your dog entirely, a situation which it will quickly learn to exploit.

It is so important in the early, formative months that the young dog is not exposed to situations which are likely to inculcate bad habits. Do not expose it to the embarrassment of ill-trained dogs, which run-in and indulge in every vice in the book. It requires only a momentary lapse of attention on your part and weeks of work can be undone.

Some owners take their youngsters to clay shoots to 'teach them to get used to gunfire'. In many cases no harm will ensue, but there is always the risk that a sensitive dog will be upset by them. You would also be well advised not to take your dog to shows and country fairs. The dog will not enjoy itself. Obviously, it is a different matter if you are running a dog in a test or scurry.

# 11  Testing times

The gundog test has emerged as an off-season activity which provides a great deal of pleasure for numerous people, exercise and discipline for their dogs, and an admirable means of conveying this aspect of the field sports message to a wide audience. Nevertheless, innocuous though gundog tests may appear, they have their critics, and virulent and vehement some of them are too in their condemnation. The crux of their argument is that certain gundog owners are taking tests so seriously that a breed of test-orientated gundog is emerging, a dog that would be virtually lost in the shooting field proper, but which is adept at finding and retrieving dummies under a variety of moderately testing conditions. It is, for obvious reasons, impractical to simulate a running, wounded bird in a test and the critics claim that tests are merely encouraging a fast, galloping dog which barely uses its nose and relies to a great extent on its handler's directions. In other words, it is beginning to lose its sense of initiative.

Well, there is a case to be answered here, but the benefit derived from tests probably outweighs the harm. It is the pot-hunting fanatic who is likely to cause the damage, not the average owner who can see that these summer tests are just that and no more; an occasion to be enjoyed and not taken too desperately seriously.

Working tests developed as a result of the establishment of training classes organized by various breed societies. Peter Moxon, a doyen of gundog instructors and trainers, was instrumental in encouraging the movement in the early 1950s. Initially he was asked to act as instructor to training classes for the United Retriever Club in Kent, and such was the enthusiasm, so great the numbers who attended the classes, and so variable their degrees of ability that it was found essential to provide some sort of final exam or test at the end of the course. From this developed the gundog test as we know it today.

Gundog tests play an important part not only in presenting the case for field sports, but also in helping to introduce newcomers to the world of gundogs and shooting. Many people, having discovered the pleasures of working dogs under artificial conditions, decide to go on to shooting proper, or trials, or both.

Tests can be divided into those which are designed almost as a set-piece for some country occasion, the Game Fair being the prime example; and those which are run on a club basis. The object in both cases is to try, as far as possible, to provide a series of exercises involving the use of dummies, occasionally cold game, and distractions such as live pigeon released from traps and artificial rabbits which whistle past the dog's nose. There are usually one or two judges, though a major event may have up to four. There will be stewards, dummy throwers and one or more assistants armed with guns loaded with blanks.

Exercises will consist of straightforward retrieves of single dummies, perhaps with a fence to jump, two dummies to be retrieved in order, and a water test. For retrievers such a test, given even a flat field adjacent to a pool or lake, is relatively simple to organize, but for spaniels the complication of hunting cover adds a dimension which is not always successfully overcome. For HPRs it becomes even more difficult, expected as they are to point pigeon imprisoned in cages and tucked into a pile of brushwood. Sometimes it works, but many times the test fails. And although the audience, if there is one, may find it amusing to see a dog and handler making fools of themselves, neither enjoys it nor does it do the breed any good. Tests, if they are to have a public audience, must be carefully thought out; there are so many factors to consider – can the audience see every exercise? Is the course sufficiently testing yet not so daunting that dog after dog is going to fail? Will it produce dogwork which will demonstrate to the audience the abilities of a particular breed?

Working tests organized for the benefit of club members are not so demanding. Dogs running in them should be at the stage when they would have finished their basic training and be on the point of entering the shooting field proper. They will be capable of being handled on to retrieves on land and water, be able to jump, will demonstrate some ability to hunt if called upon to do so and will, of course, exhibit no signs of gunshyness or tendency to run-in. If there is some form of distraction they will remain staunch. Tests cannot, of course, reveal whether a dog has any tendency to hard mouth, nor whether it is capable of taking the line of a runner under a variety of scenting conditions. Only a field trial or shooting proper can reveal these aspects.

Once a dog has been entered to the real thing, it will probably show a reduced enthusiasm for what it can only regard as a pale imitation. Tests should really only be for young dogs as a summer finishing school. They should not be taken too seriously, and treated with a degree of irreverence they can be great fun. Do not become uptight about them or worry unduly if your dog misbehaves; it's not the end of the world. Try to relax and keep your handling to the bare minimum. Arm-waving and frantic whistling and shouting will only confuse the dog and convince the judge that it is you, not the dog, which is at fault.

Do not imagine that just because your youngster has fared well in a few tests in the summer, it can be entered directly into the world of field trials. There is a wealth of difference between the two, and the dog should only be considered for the trial world after it has gained experience of the shooting field and proved itself there.

# Index